W9-CSL-399
This book belongs to
Shravya

Illumisaurus

WIDE EYED EDITIONS

by

Carnovsky

written by

Lucy Brownridge

welcome to the world of the dinosaurs

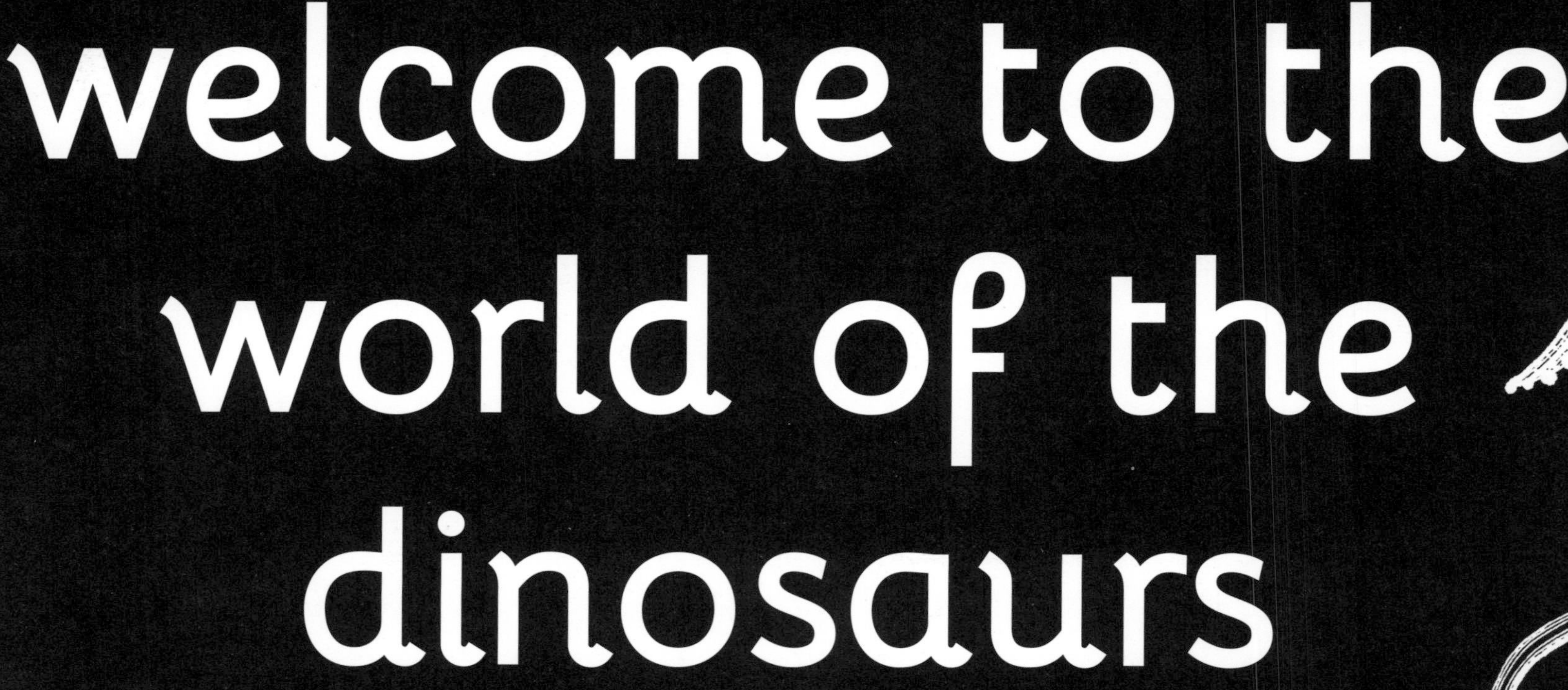

The earth beneath our feet is a time capsule. Take your *palaeontology lens* to draw back the veil of time and reveal the dinosaurs that once roamed our planet. The ground below us stores the *bones* and *fossils* and *petrified remains* of *prehistoric life* in treasure-like hoards. Get ready to journey back millennia to when dry land was a single, connected mass called *Pangaea*. Watch as it drifts apart over time, nourishing and sustaining powerful dinosaurs, luscious plants, bountiful blossoms and unusual, early mammals. Visit every corner of the globe and see *where in the world* the most famous dinosaurs lived. Step onto *the observation deck* and meet the rich cast of dinosaurs, plants and other prehistoric animals from each place. Learn more about them in the palaeontologist's *species guide.*

What will you discover on your prehistoric adventure around the globe?

CONTENTS

Take a trip around the prehistoric planet.

HOW TO USE THIS BOOK

WHERE IN THE WORLD

Visit a ***part of the world***, see the lie of the land and discover what a dinosaur habitat would have been like.

THE OBSERVATION DECK

Step on to the ***observation deck***. Tread carefully and watch out for dangerous dinosaurs, ancient plants and unusual creatures.

SPECIES GUIDE

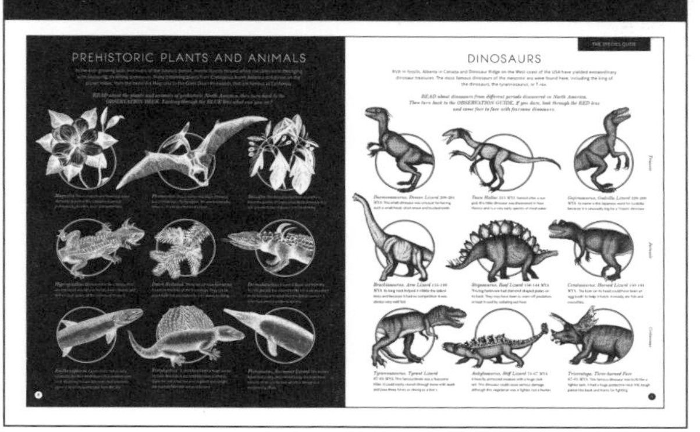

Then, turn the page to learn more about each species, the meaning behind each dinosaur's name and how many million years ago it lived (MYA) in the ***species guide***.

Use the ***red*** lens to reveal the dinosaurs or "terrible lizards" that would have lived in each location.

Look through the ***green*** lens to see the location.

Look through the ***blue*** lens to uncover the plants and prehistoric animals that would have inhabited this place.

THE WORLD

The dinosaurs lived during a time we call the Mesozoic era, which lasted for 186 million years. Scientists split the long Mesozoic era into three stages: the Triassic, Jurassic, and Cretaceous periods. Over these periods the world map would have looked very different to the one we recognize today. This is because the Earth's crust is split into big chunks, called tectonic plates, that travel apart very slowly. They are moved by the swirling molten lava beneath them.

The land was once a huge, joined-up super-continent, but over time it split up into the smaller continents we know today. The continents are still drifting apart at a rate of 1 inch per year.

TRIASSIC PERIOD

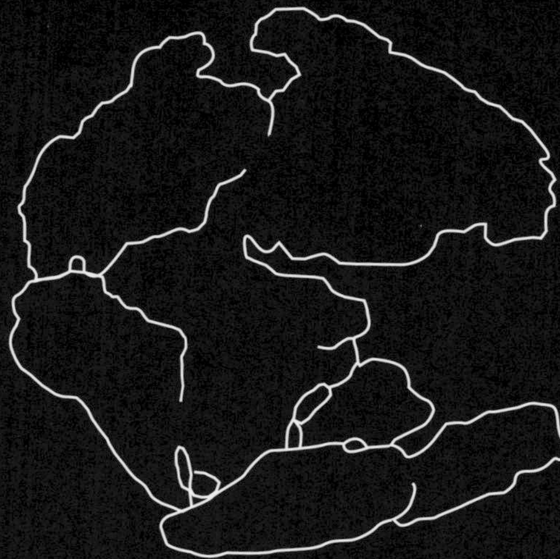

In the Triassic period, the land on Earth was all squashed together in one big super-continent called Pangaea. The word is made from the two Greek words: "pan" which means whole and "gaia" which means land. The climate was hot and dry and there were no ice caps. Pangaea was home to the first dinosaurs. There were few of them and they were small. At the end of this period, the land began to split apart.

JURASSIC PERIOD

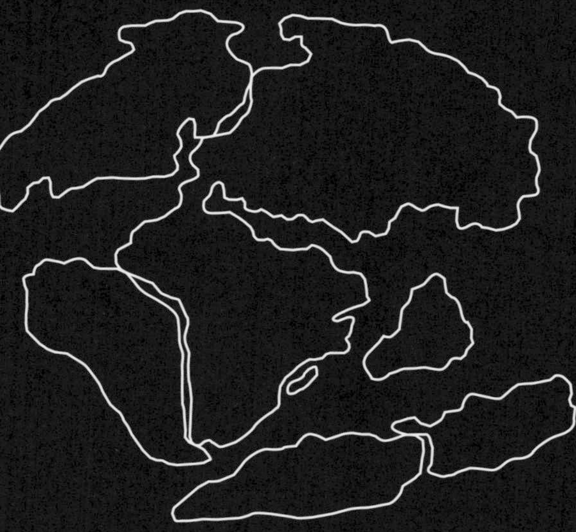

In the Jurassic period, the land roughly split into two, creating Laurasia in the north and Gondwana in the south. The climate cooled and there was a lot more rain. Because the land was no longer hot and dry, new plants began to flourish and plant-eating dinosaurs could grow bigger. By the end of the Jurassic period, giant sauropods ruled the plains and chomped through lush forests.

CRETACEOUS PERIOD

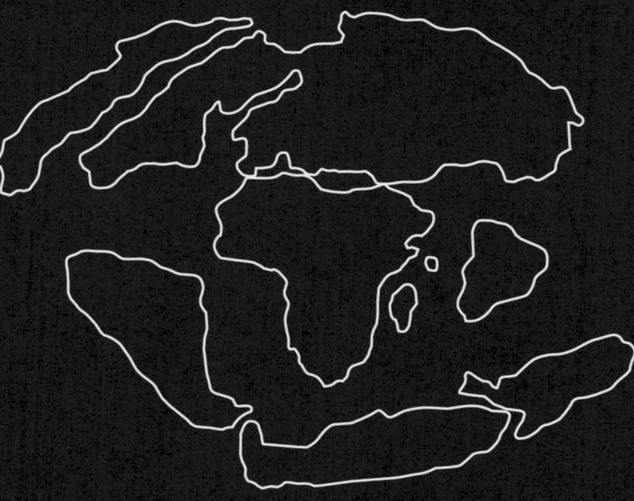

This is known as the golden age of dinosaurs. By this time, the continents had drifted apart significantly. Dinosaurs started to change to suit their climate, environment, and the other plants and animals they lived along side. Flowering plants bloomed for the first time, and pollinating insects such as bees began to buzz around the lush forests.

PREHISTORIC PLANTS AND ANIMALS

Many insects and animals from the Triassic period perished in a mass extinction. Plants in Jurassic times grew taller as the growing oceans around the land made more rain fall. By the Cretaceous period, there were freezing temperatures at the South Pole, the first flowers graced the Earth and pollinating insects such as bees and butterflies appeared.

READ about the key species of plants and animals from each of the three periods, then turn back to the OBSERVATION DECK. Looking through the BLUE lens, what can you see?

Triassic

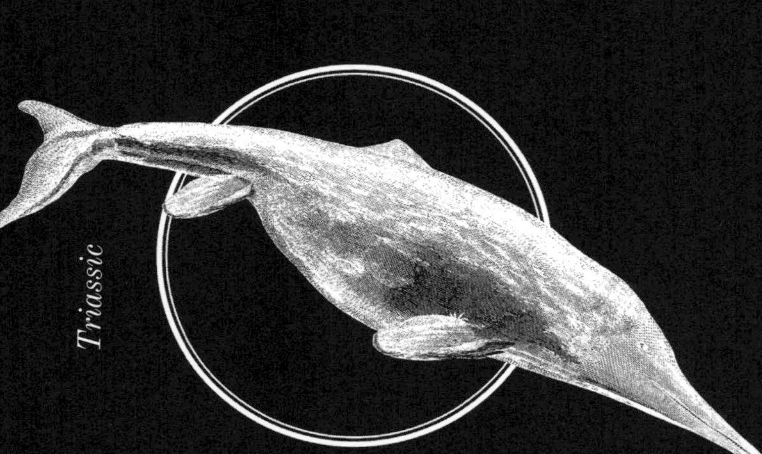

Ichthyosaurus This was a family of underwater reptiles that included this *Shonisaurus* and looked a lot like fish.

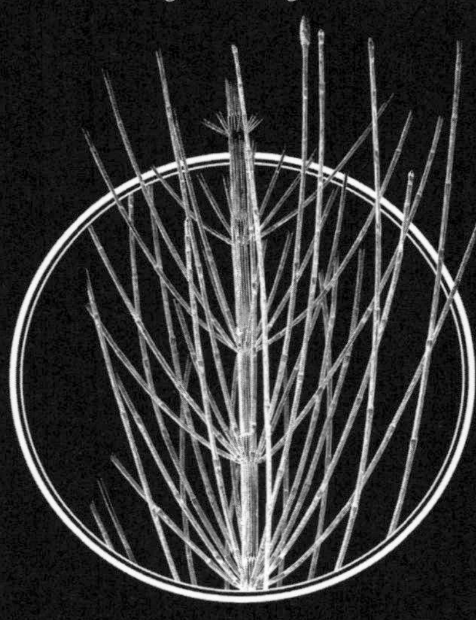

Horsetails These curious plants would have been a large part of the vegetation in the early Triassic period. They are still around today.

Therapsids There were few dinosaurs at this time but many mammal-like therapsids, such as this *Cynognathus*, roamed Pangaea.

Jurassic

Lush forest As the climate dropped and more rain fell, big lush forests popped up with unusual trees like this monkey puzzle tree.

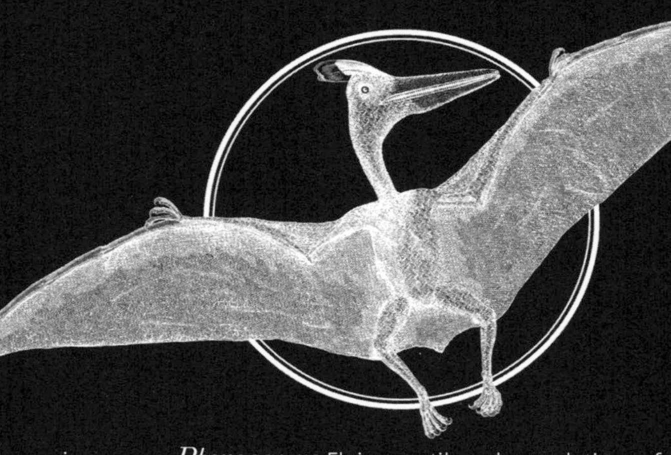

Pterosaurs Flying reptiles, close relatives of dinosaurs, such as this *Kryptodrakon* started to dominate the Jurassic skies.

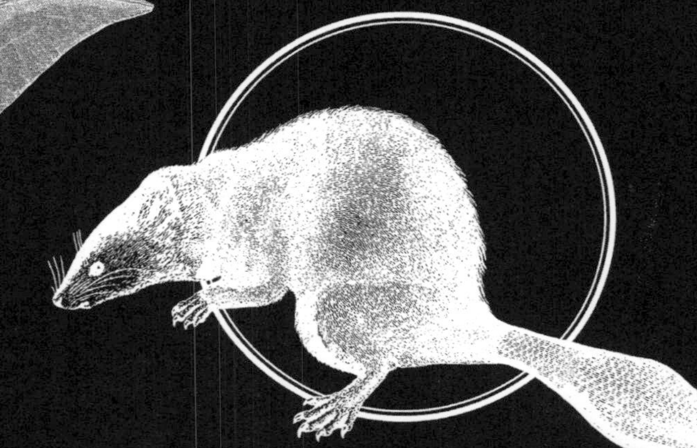

Swimming mammals Semi-aquatic mammals like this *Castorocauda* started to appear as the diversity of mammal forms began to explode.

Cretaceous

Pollinating insects These insect newcomers such as nectar-sucking butterflies were critical to the arrival of flowering plants.

Flowering plants such as the tulip tree would have been pollinated by nectar-sucking butterflies and started blooming all over the planet.

Broad-leaved trees Trees with big leaves, rather than fine needles, like this plane tree started to appear and provided heartier meals for big hungry sauropods.

DINOSAURS

In Triassic times, dinosaurs were relatively small and only made up a small part of life on Earth. After a mass extinction event at the end of the Triassic period the dinosaurs were some of the main survivors and they became more dominant. More diverse species appeared over time as the landmasses drifted apart and they had to adapt to different climates, food, and predators. But by the end of the Cretaceous period, dinosaurs had truly conquered every continent.

READ about the key dinosaur developments from different periods around the world. Then turn back to the OBSERVATION DECK. Look through the RED lens and come face to face with the dinosaurs you have learned about.

Triassic

Sauropodomorph One of the first groups of dinosaur and this *Saturnalia* is thought to have been one of the earliest.

Ornithischians *Pisanosaurus* was one of the first ornithschians and only evolved in the late Triassic period.

Small theropods The first meat-eating dinosaurs like this *Coelophysis* would have mostly been small scavengers.

Jurassic

Big sauropods As trees grew taller, so did plant-eating sauropods like this *Diplodocus* so that they could reach the highest leaves.

Bird-like theropods Some theropods started to look more like birds. This feathered *Anchiornis* grew wings and feathers but would not have been able to fly.

Carnivorous theropods This was the age of the terrifying meat-eaters. They developed bigger bodies, strong leg muscles and this *Yangchuanosaurus* would have had a keen sense of smell.

Cretaceous

Intimidating herbivores Frilled dinosaurs like the *Styracosaurus* would have been spoiling for a fight and were deliberately frilly to look intimidating.

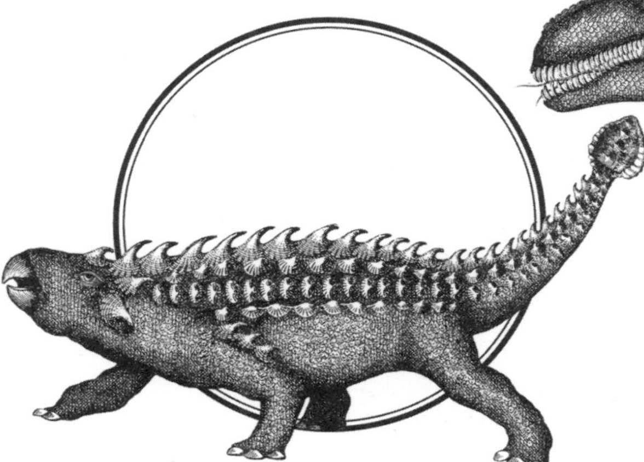

Defensive plant-eaters To protect themselves from predators, herbivores started to grow their own suits of armour, like the *Euoplocephalus* which had a club tail and spikes all over its body.

Gigantic predators As prey developed better armor, predators had to become specialized killing machines like this ultra-tough *Carcharodontosaurus*.

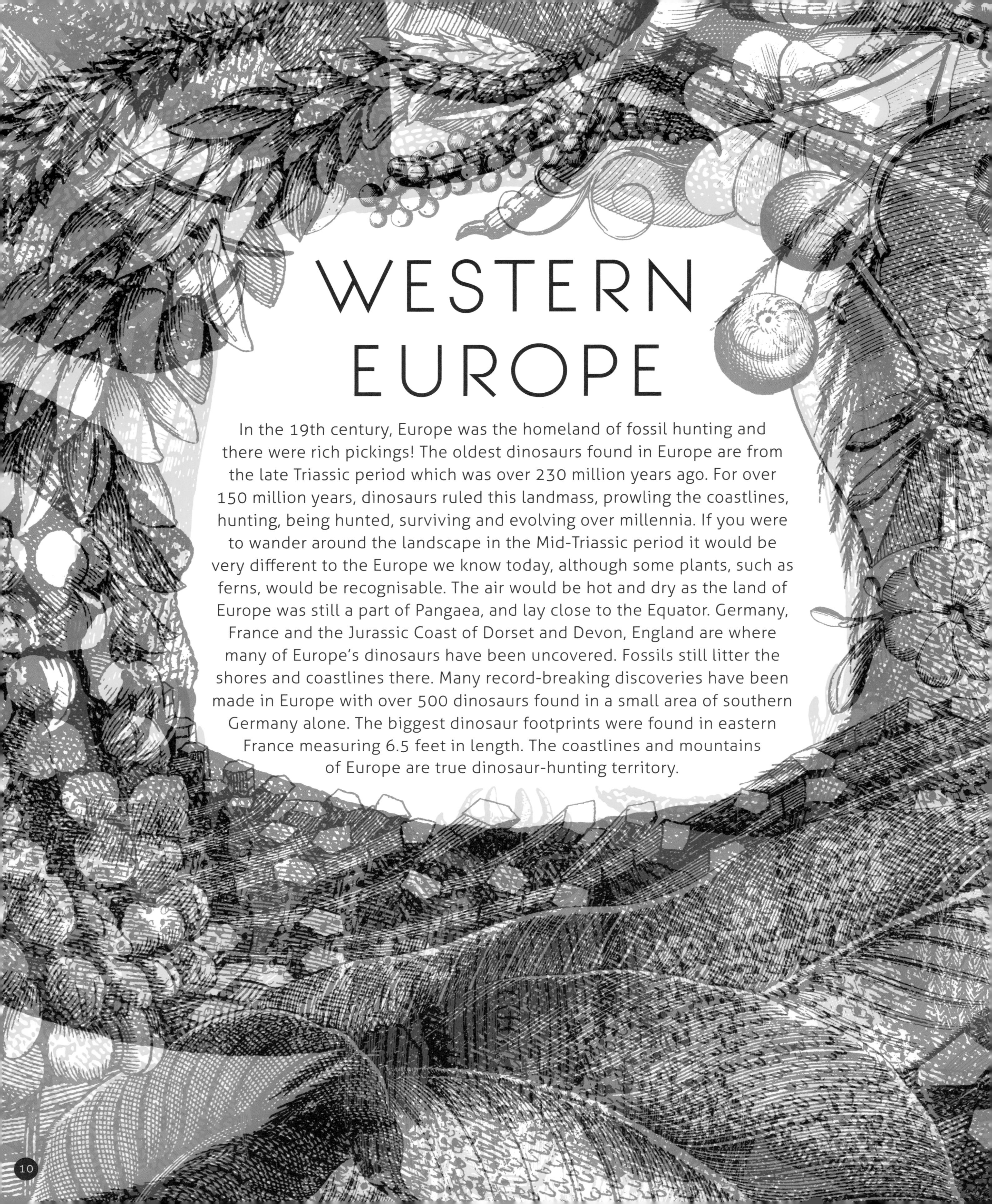

WESTERN EUROPE

In the 19th century, Europe was the homeland of fossil hunting and there were rich pickings! The oldest dinosaurs found in Europe are from the late Triassic period which was over 230 million years ago. For over 150 million years, dinosaurs ruled this landmass, prowling the coastlines, hunting, being hunted, surviving and evolving over millennia. If you were to wander around the landscape in the Mid-Triassic period it would be very different to the Europe we know today, although some plants, such as ferns, would be recognisable. The air would be hot and dry as the land of Europe was still a part of Pangaea, and lay close to the Equator. Germany, France and the Jurassic Coast of Dorset and Devon, England are where many of Europe's dinosaurs have been uncovered. Fossils still litter the shores and coastlines there. Many record-breaking discoveries have been made in Europe with over 500 dinosaurs found in a small area of southern Germany alone. The biggest dinosaur footprints were found in eastern France measuring 6.5 feet in length. The coastlines and mountains of Europe are true dinosaur-hunting territory.

WELCOME TO WESTERN EUROPE
1
2
3
4
5
6
7
8
9
DINOSAUR DISCOVERY SITES
1 Plateosaurus, Germany
2 Liliensternus, Germany
3 Saltopus, Scotland, UK
4 Megalosaurus, England, UK
5 Archaeopteryx, Germany
6 Juravenator, Germany
7 Baryonyx, England, UK
8 Eotyrannus, Isle of Wight, UK
9 Iguanodon, Belgium

PREHISTORIC PLANTS AND ANIMALS

During the Mesozoic era, Western Europe was a land of plenty with many thriving ecosystems. Its busy waterways were filled with strange fish, its oceans teemed with ancient sharks, and the land was home to many early mammals, insects, and plants that we still see around us today. Even now, you can hunt for fossils in Western Europe and find incredible imprints of ancient life.

READ about the plants and animals of prehistoric Western Europe, then turn back to the OBSERVATION DECK. Looking through the BLUE lens, what can you see?

Ardeosaurus Discovered in the south of Germany, this ancient lizard is an ancestor of the gecko. It had a flat head and a long slender body.

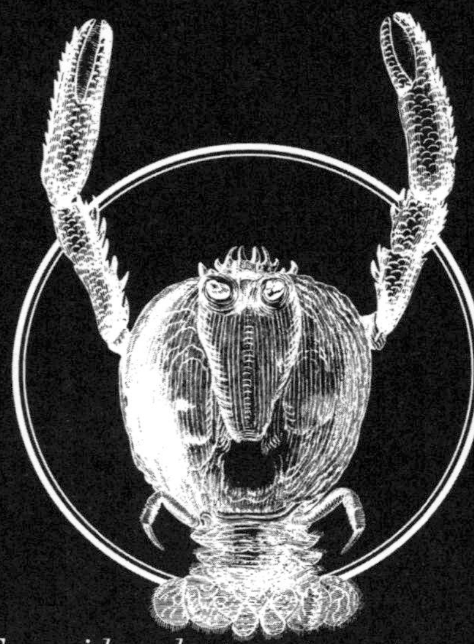

Eryonid crab A long-pincered, snapping crab from late Jurassic times. A pristine fossil was discovered in Germany.

Oak tree In the Cretaceous period, broad-leaved trees like the oak began to appear, providing big, delicious leaves and nuts for plant-eaters.

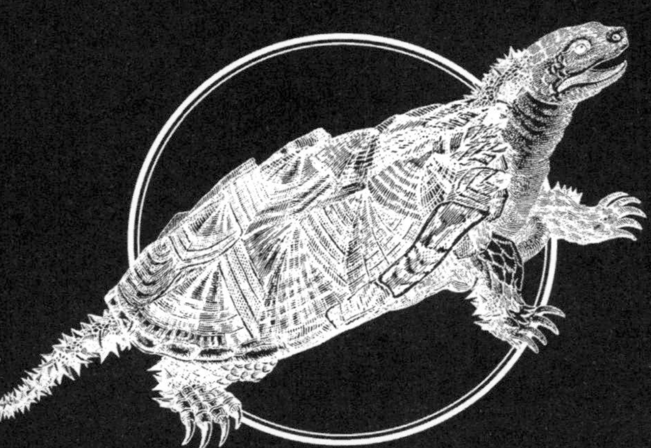

Proganochelys One of the earliest types of turtle ever found, with protective plates on top of and underneath its body, as well as down its legs.

Dragonfly These beautiful insects lived long before the dinosaurs and their descendants still dart across the tops of ponds today.

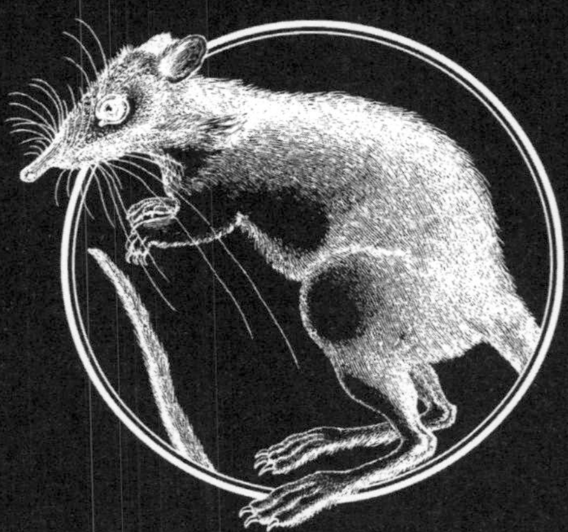

Leptictidium Its name means "graceful weasel" in Ancient Greek! This mammal looked a little like a shrew and would have run around on its hind legs.

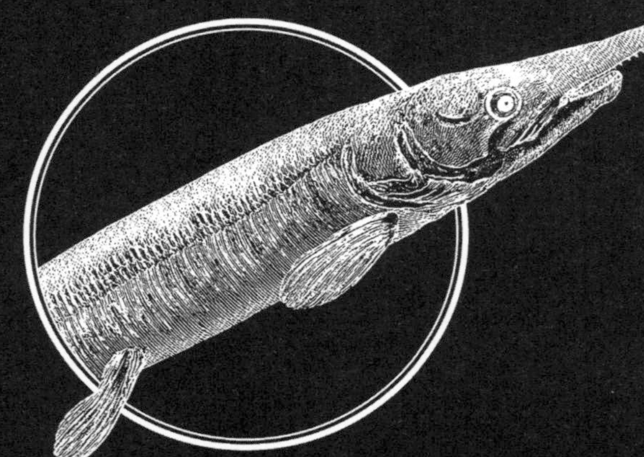

Aspidorhynchus A ray-finned fish from the Jurassic and Cretaceous periods, it had sharp teeth and would have been a fast swimmer.

Peony Eudicot flowers such as this peony started to bloom in the late Cretaceous period. They are in the same family as sunflowers and dandelions.

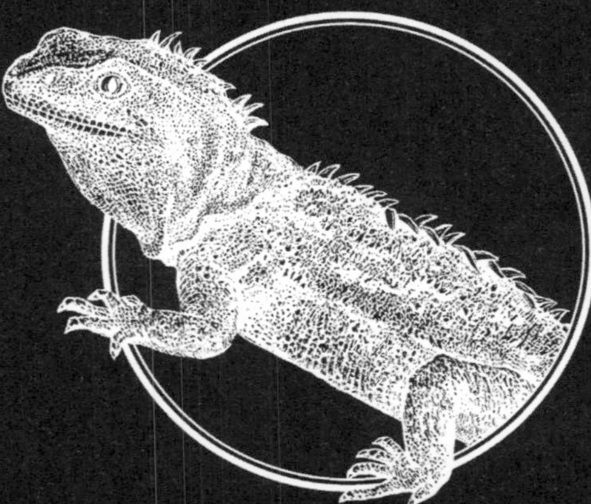

Planocephalosaurus It was found in Europe and its descendant, the tuatara, still lives in New Zealand to this day, 220 million years later.

DINOSAURS

It is on this continent that dinosaur bones were first studied by scientists. In southern Germany and along the south coast of England, there are still swathes of exposed prehistoric rock. It is hard to imagine, but dinosaurs would have lived all over this continent and would have walked on the earth now buried beneath big towns and cities.

READ about dinosaurs from different periods discovered in Western Europe. Then turn back to the OBSERVATION DECK. If you dare, look through the RED lens and come face to face with fearsome dinosaurs.

Triassic

Plateosaurus, Broad Lizard, 220 MYA Fossilized remains of lots of these plant-eaters were found together which shows that they moved in herds.

Liliensternus, for Liliensterns, 205-202 MYA This early predator was lightweight and speedy. It had two fins on the top of its snout and sharp teeth.

Saltopus, Hopping Foot, 230 MYA This bouncy dinosaur lived in what is now Scotland and was one of the smallest carnivorous dinosaurs.

Jurassic

Megalosaurus, Big Lizard, 170 MYA One of the first dinosaurs discovered, this giant carnivore would have stalked the British coastline.

Archaeopteryx, Ancient Wing, 147 MYA This pint-sized predator had wings but lived 70 million years before the first modern bird evolved.

Juravenator, Bavarian Hunter, 150 MYA A chicken-sized, meat-eating dinosaur with feathers and lizard-like scales.

Cretaceous

Baryonyx, Heavy Claw, 125 MYA This 10-metre-long carnivore had jaws like a crocodile and roamed the riverbanks of Surrey, England!

Eotyrannus, Dawn Tyrant, 127-121 MYA Discovered on the coast of the Isle of Wight, this was an early and small form of tyrannosaur.

Iguanodon, Iguana Tooth, 140-110 MYA This dinosaur could choose to walk on four legs or upright on two. It had a big spike on its hand to jab any predators that came too close.

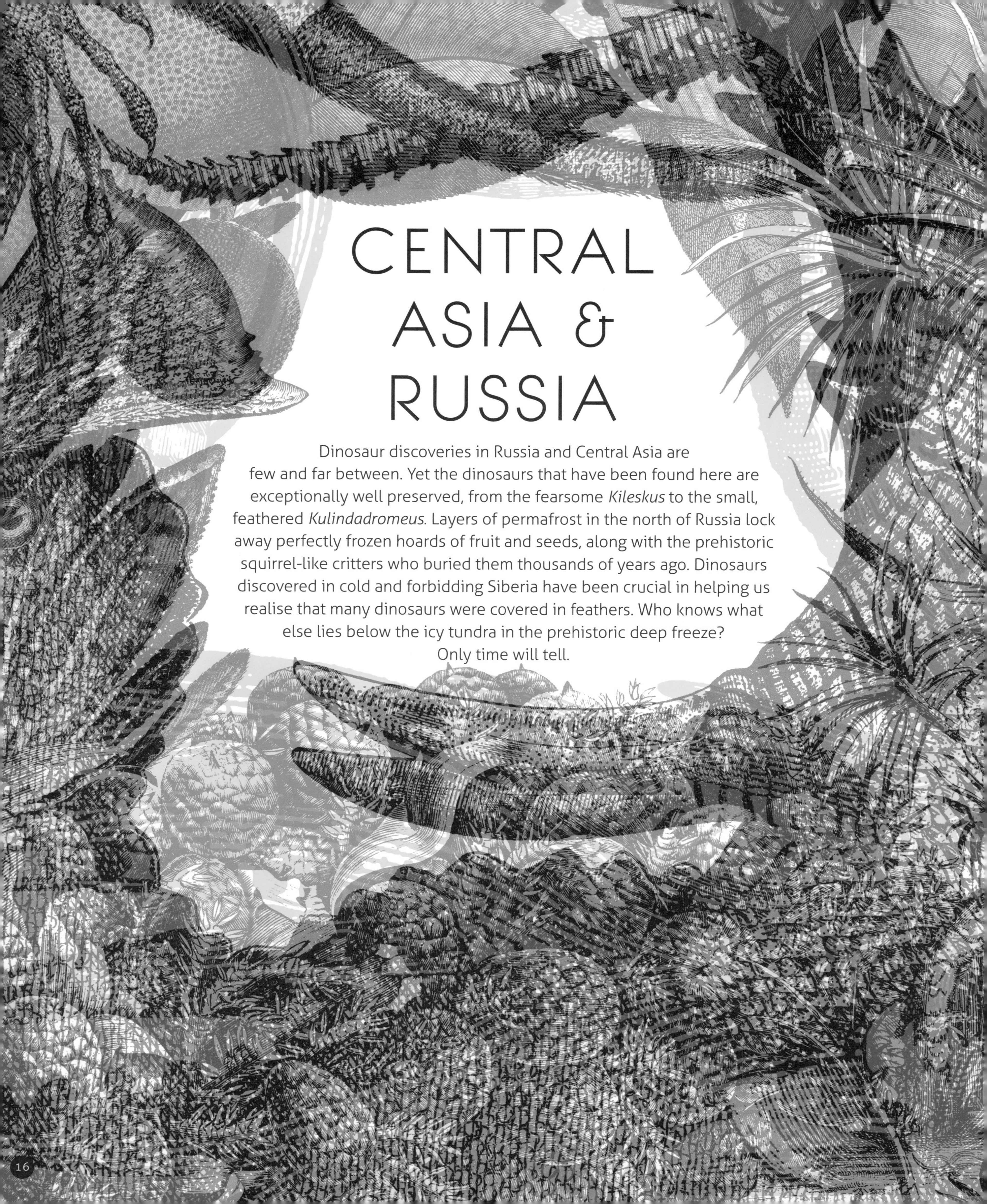

CENTRAL ASIA & RUSSIA

Dinosaur discoveries in Russia and Central Asia are few and far between. Yet the dinosaurs that have been found here are exceptionally well preserved, from the fearsome *Kileskus* to the small, feathered *Kulindadromeus*. Layers of permafrost in the north of Russia lock away perfectly frozen hoards of fruit and seeds, along with the prehistoric squirrel-like critters who buried them thousands of years ago. Dinosaurs discovered in cold and forbidding Siberia have been crucial in helping us realise that many dinosaurs were covered in feathers. Who knows what else lies below the icy tundra in the prehistoric deep freeze? Only time will tell.

WELCOME TO
CENTRAL ASIA & RUSSIA
1
2
3
4
5
6
7
8
9
DINOSAUR DISCOVERY SITES
1 *Kileskus*, Krasnoyarsk Krai, Russia
2 *Kulindadromeus*, Zabaykalsky Krai, Russia
3 *Olorotitan*, Amur, Russia
4 *Turanoceratops*, Uzbekistan
5 *Urbacodon*, Uzbekistan
6 *Sibirotitan*, western Siberia, Russia
7 *Aralosaurus*, Kazakhstan
8 *Psittacosaurus*, western Siberia, Russia
9 *Erectopus*, south west Russia

PREHISTORIC PLANTS AND ANIMALS

Remains of many prehistoric plants and animals found in this part of the world are from a time long before the dinosaurs first started to appear. A hoard of fossils unearthed in Uzbekistan revealed amazing new evidence of fish, frogs, and ancient sharks, showing that it would have once been a watery wonderland. In the tundra, ancient seeds have defrosted and in some cases, been brought to life!

READ about the plants and animals of prehistoric Central Asia and Russia, then turn back to the OBSERVATION DECK. Looking through the BLUE lens, what can you see?

Ammonite These ancient ocean creatures had soft, squid-like bodies protected by a hard outer shell. Their shell prints are all that remain in fossils.

Arctic dock Millions of years old, seeds from these flowers have been discovered under 230 feet of icy tundra and successfully grown.

Sea star A simple but beautiful life form that has lurked at the bottom of the ocean for well over 500 million years.

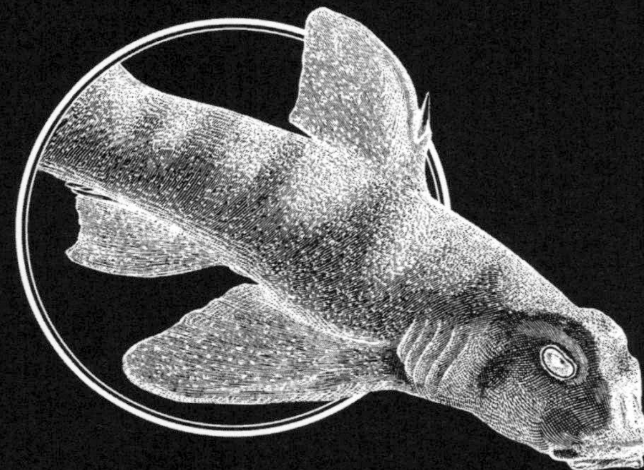

Horn shark A very old variety of shark that still swims today. It lays eggs that look like land mines!

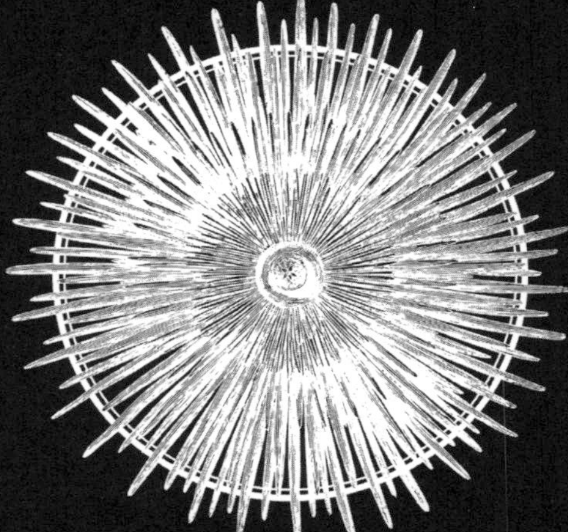

Sea urchin Creatures like this have lived in the ocean for over 450 million years and you can still see them in tide pools now!

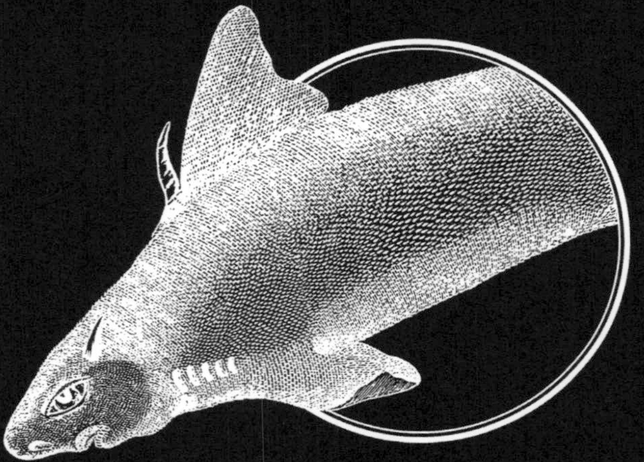

Hybodus This fish's name means humped tooth and it looked a lot like a shark. It would have patroled the ocean depths 300 million years ago.

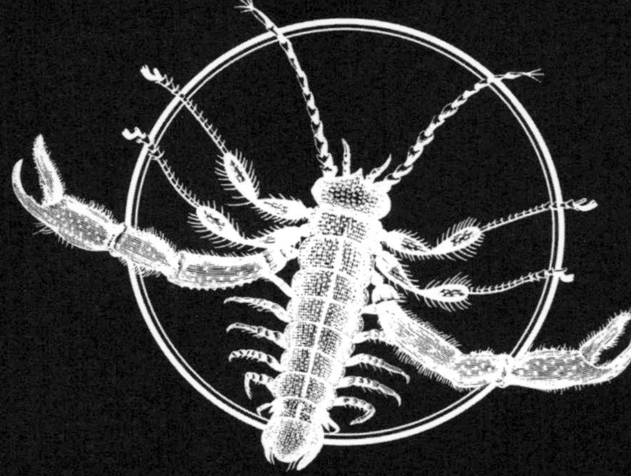

Strashila incredibilis A wingless insect from Jurassic Siberia. Its fossil looks like it is defending itself so its name means "incredibly frightened."

Narrow-leaved campion 40,000 year old seeds from this plant were discovered under ice, stored in a frozen, ancient squirrel's burrow.

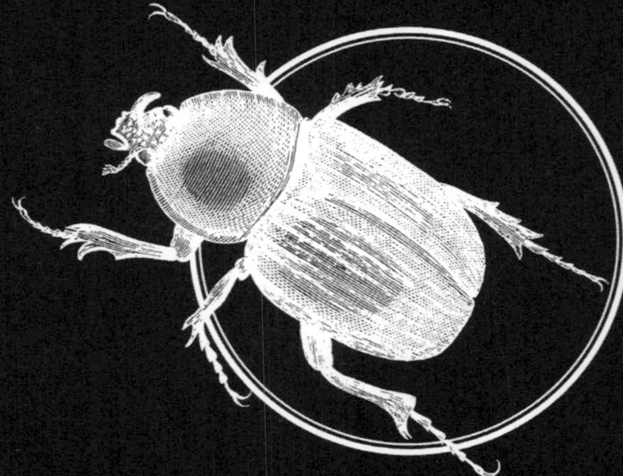

Dung beetle These familiar bugs appeared on Earth in the early Cretaceous period at the time when life forms began to diversify faster than ever.

DINOSAURS

The Siberian chill factor has prevented dinosaur hunters from finding much treasure in Russia and Central Asia. But this place didn't always have such a forbidding climate. It used to be home to many feathered, plant-eating dinosaurs that roamed lush forests. It is bitter-sweet that as global warming melts the permafrost, we may start to discover more and more species of dinosaur, buried beneath the ice in these regions.

READ about dinosaurs from different periods discovered in Central Asia and Russia. Then turn back to the OBSERVATION DECK. If you dare, look through the RED lens and come face to face with fearsome dinosaurs.

Jurassic

Kileskus, 165 MYA A less intimidating member of the tyrannosaur family, it would have been covered in a layer of fuzz to keep warm.

Jurassic

Kulindadromeus, Kulinda Runner, 174-145 MYA A tiny dinosaur with "protofeathers" which were scale-like early versions of feathers.

Cretaceous

Olorotitan, Titanic Swan, 70-66 MYA A duck-billed dinosaur discovered in the south east of Russia. It had a unique, hollow crest on its head.

Turanoceratops, Turan Horned Face, 90 MYA Its name is a give away but this dinosaur charged around with a seriously weaponized face.

Urbacodon, Urbac Tooth, 95 MYA A feathered carnivore that is unusual in its family for having blunt teeth rather than sharp and serrated.

Cretaceous

Sibirotitan, Siberian Giant, 120 MYA Discovered in frosty Siberia, it would have been super tall and is the oldest titanosaur found in Asia.

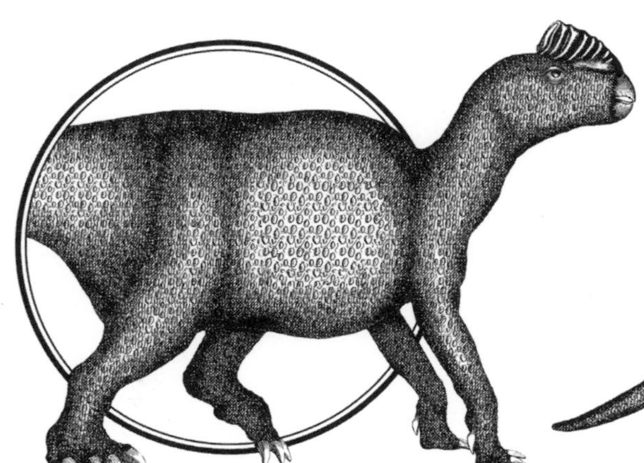

Aralosaurus, Aral Lizard, 94-84 MYA Found in Kazakhstan. This beaked dinosaur roamed central Asia with a big crest of bone on its nose, perfect for head-butting its rivals.

Psittacosaurus, Parrot Lizard, 120-100 MYA Best known from China, specimens were also found in Russia in 2014; it sported a remarkable set of porcupine-like bristles along its back.

Erectopus, Upright Foot, 129 MYA A carnivorous dinosaur that would have stood on two legs, and reached waist height next to a human.

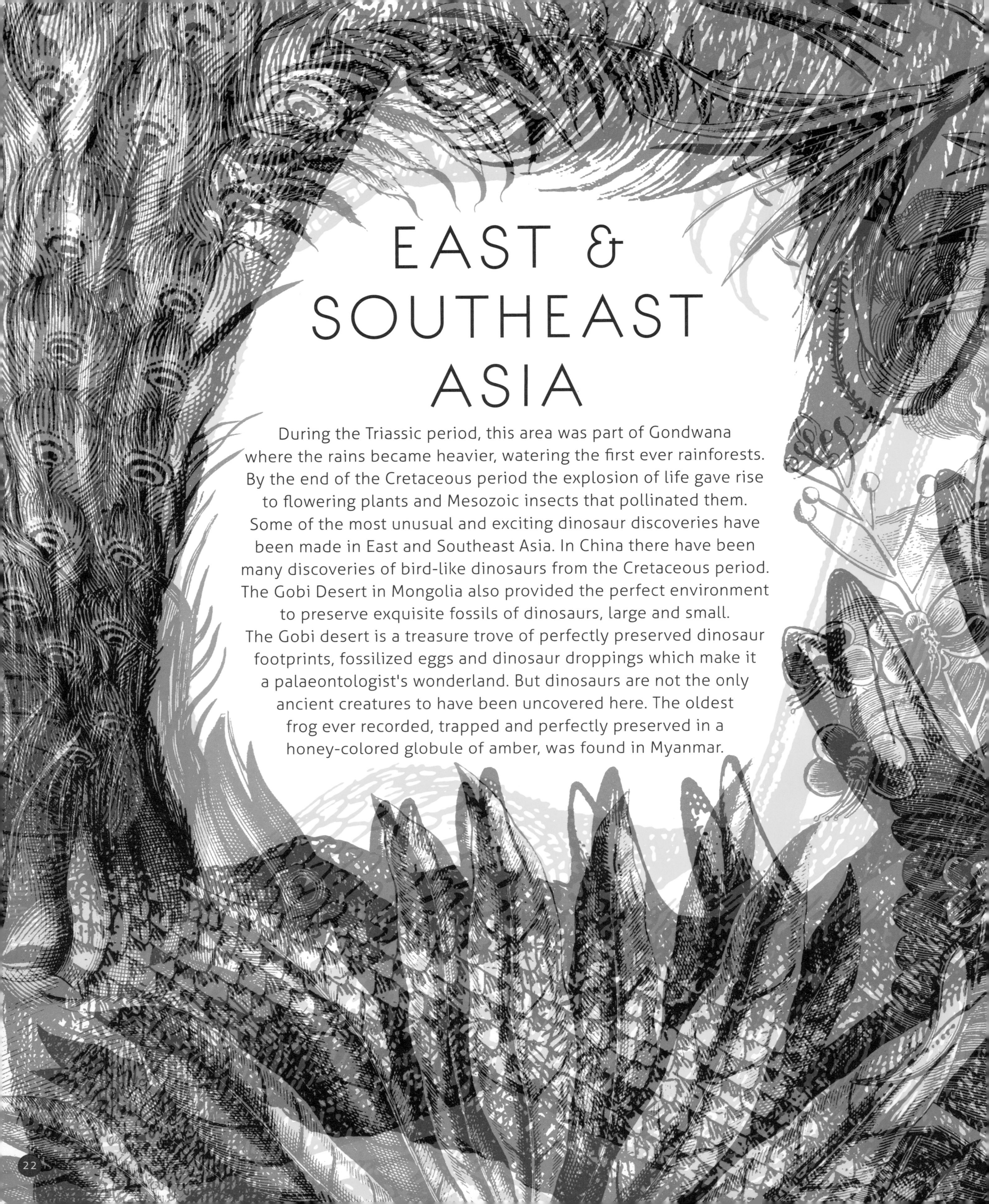

EAST & SOUTHEAST ASIA

During the Triassic period, this area was part of Gondwana where the rains became heavier, watering the first ever rainforests. By the end of the Cretaceous period the explosion of life gave rise to flowering plants and Mesozoic insects that pollinated them. Some of the most unusual and exciting dinosaur discoveries have been made in East and Southeast Asia. In China there have been many discoveries of bird-like dinosaurs from the Cretaceous period. The Gobi Desert in Mongolia also provided the perfect environment to preserve exquisite fossils of dinosaurs, large and small. The Gobi desert is a treasure trove of perfectly preserved dinosaur footprints, fossilized eggs and dinosaur droppings which make it a palaeontologist's wonderland. But dinosaurs are not the only ancient creatures to have been uncovered here. The oldest frog ever recorded, trapped and perfectly preserved in a honey-colored globule of amber, was found in Myanmar.

WELCOME TO EAST & SOUTHEAST ASIA
9
7
8
4
5
6
2
3
1
DINOSAUR DISCOVERY SITES
1 Isanosaurus, Thailand
2 Sinosaurus, Yunnan, China
3 Lufengosaurus, Yunnan, China
4 Epidexipteryx, Hebei, China
5 Chungkingosaurus, Sichuan, China
6 Agilosaurus, Sichuan, China
7 Nomingia, Mongolia
8 Gigantoraptor, Mongolia
9 Linhenykus, Mongolia

PREHISTORIC PLANTS AND ANIMALS

Extraordinary plants and animals hailed from this part of the prehistoric world. Many plants from millennia ago are still in forests, ornamental gardens, and used in cooking and perfumes today. Beautiful birds preened while gliding mammals devised clever ways of escaping capture.

READ about the plants and animals of prehistoric East and Southeast Asia, then turn back to the OBSERVATION DECK. Looking through the BLUE lens, what can you see?

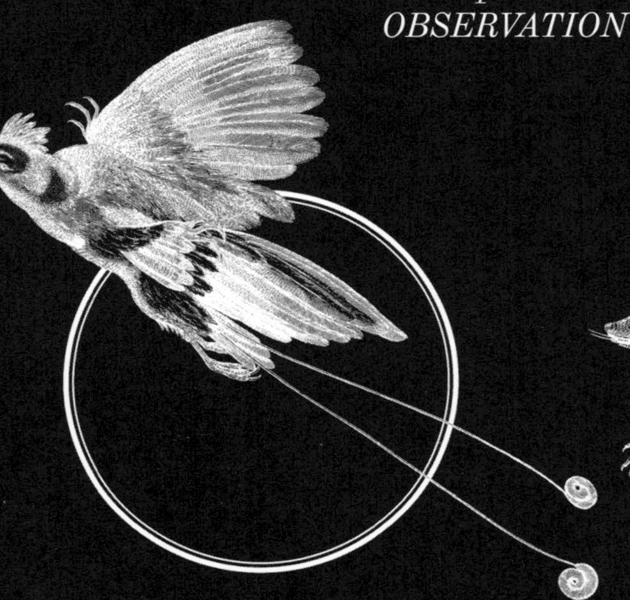

Confuciusornis An early type of bird from the Early Cretaceous period. Fossils found in China show perfect imprints of its feathers and delicate wings.

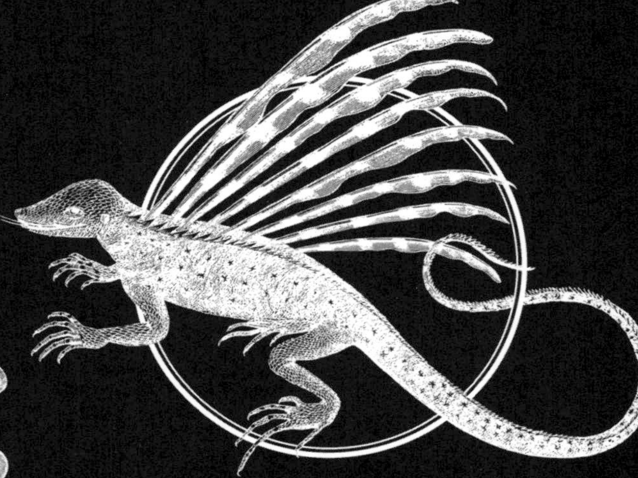

Longisquama A show-stopping lizard with exquisite fan-like scales. Some scientists think they were early types of feather.

Nothosaurus This Triassic marine reptile swam and lounged on rocks near the water. It would have had webbed toes and fingers for swimming.

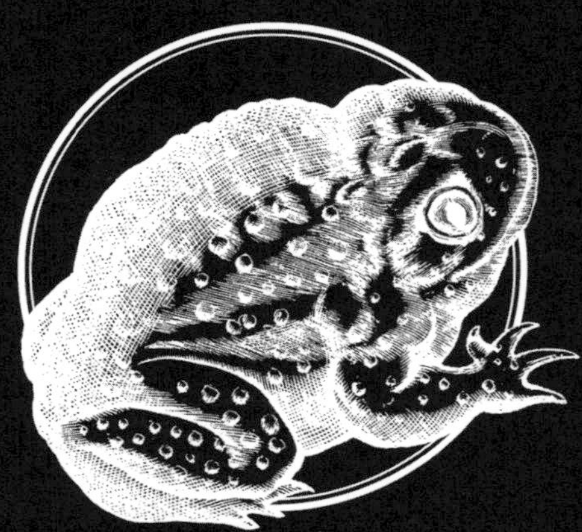

Electrorana frog The oldest known frog was found trapped in amber in Myanmar. Unlike in a fossil, you can still see its flesh and tiny veins.

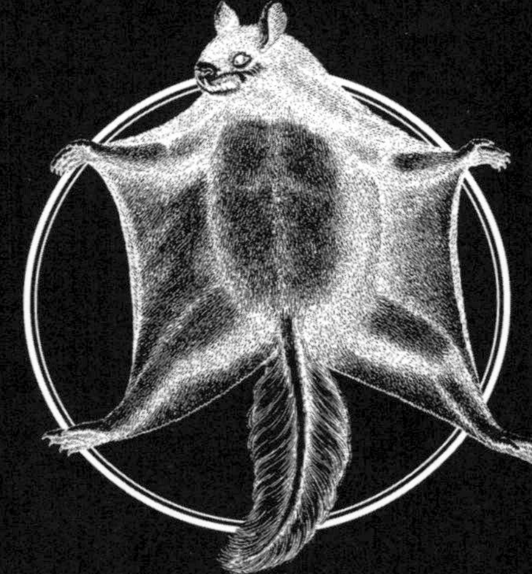

Volaticotherium A little mammal with a lot of skin! It would glide from tree to tree to stay away from dangerous dinosaurs on the forest floor.

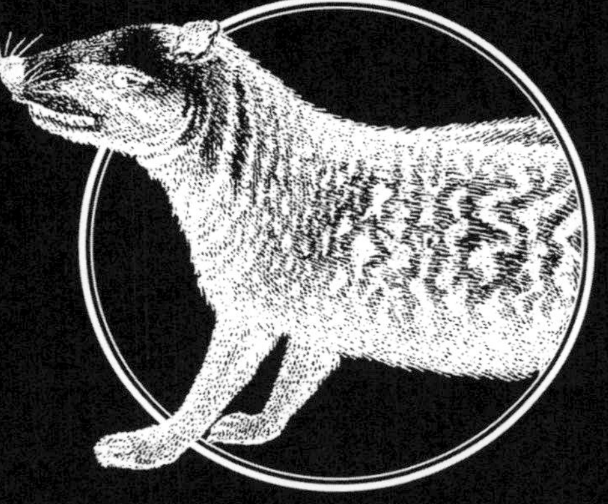

Repenomamus This giant badger-like mammal used to eat baby dinosaurs whole. Its fossil was found with a dinosaur skeleton inside its stomach.

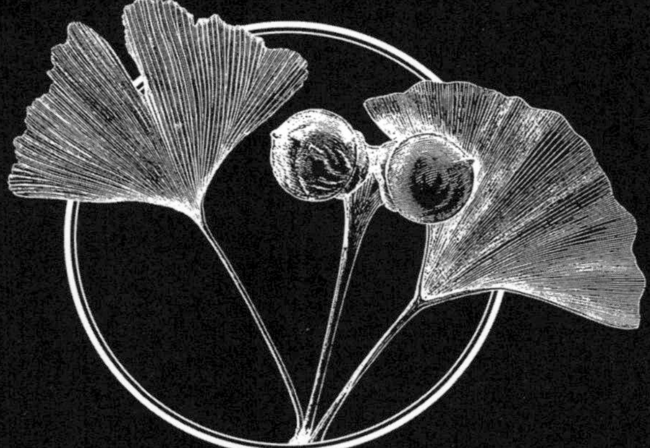

Ginkgo These beautiful trees have distinctive fan-shaped leaves. Relatives of the 140 million-year-old variety still grow today.

Juniper One of many conifer trees that would have been the main meal for most of the Jurassic herbivores. We still use its berries in drinks today.

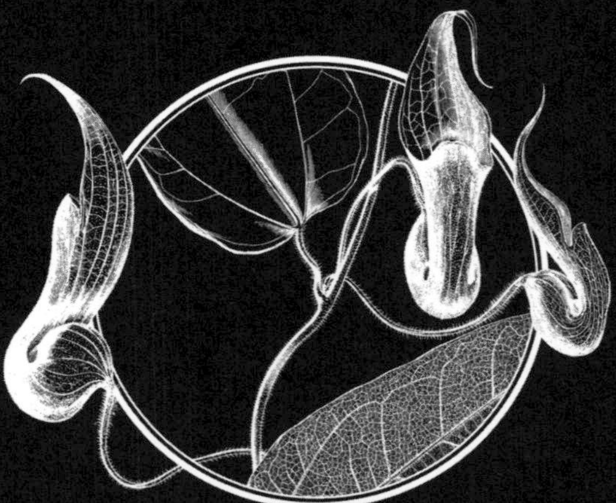

Dutchman's pipe This plant has also survived into the modern day. Its flower looks like a beautifully painted old-fashioned tobacco pipe.

DINOSAURS

Over the past 20 years, discoveries made in China have added hugely to our understanding of dinosaurs. As well as new species of dinosaur, scientists have found dinosaur droppings and dinosaur eggs with unborn foetuses still inside. Specimens like these help us to learn more about a dinosaurs life-cycle, diet and daily life.

READ about dinosaurs from different periods discovered in East and Southeast Asia. Then turn back to the OBSERVATION DECK. If you dare, look through the RED lens and come face to face with fearsome dinosaurs.

Triassic

Isanosaurus, Isan Lizard, 210 MYA Discovered in Thailand, not much of this rare and very early sauropod remains.

Sinosaurus, Chinese Lizard, 199-183 MYA It carried a crest along the top of its snout, used for signalling.

Lufengosaurus, Lufeng Lizard, 200-195 MYA This unusually tall plant-eater could stand on two legs and used its front legs to grip when eating.

Jurassic

Epidexipteryx, Display Feather, 160 MYA A tiny, early bird-like dinosaur with long tail feathers that were there just for display.

Chungkingosaurus, Chongqing Lizard, 159-142 MYA Like a Stegosaurus, it had plates along its back and a spiked tail like a mace.

Agilisaurus, Agile Lizard, 169-159 MYA This nippy beast wasn't good at fighting but could escape danger by running incredibly fast.

Cretaceous

Nomingia, 72-68 MYA This feathered dinosaur had huge and impressive tail feathers as well as well as a sharp, snapping beak.

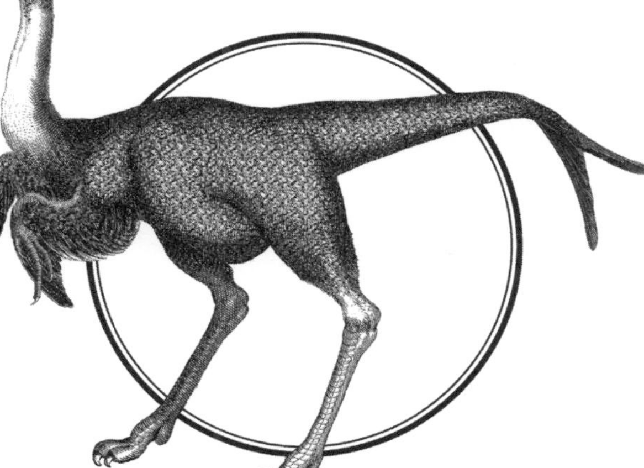

Gigantoraptor, Giant Seizer, 85 MYA A dinosaur that looked more like a giant ostrich and would have intimidated its prey.

Linhenykus, Linhe Claw, 83-72 MYA This pocket-sized dinosaur only had one finger on each arm, like two little prongs in its chest.

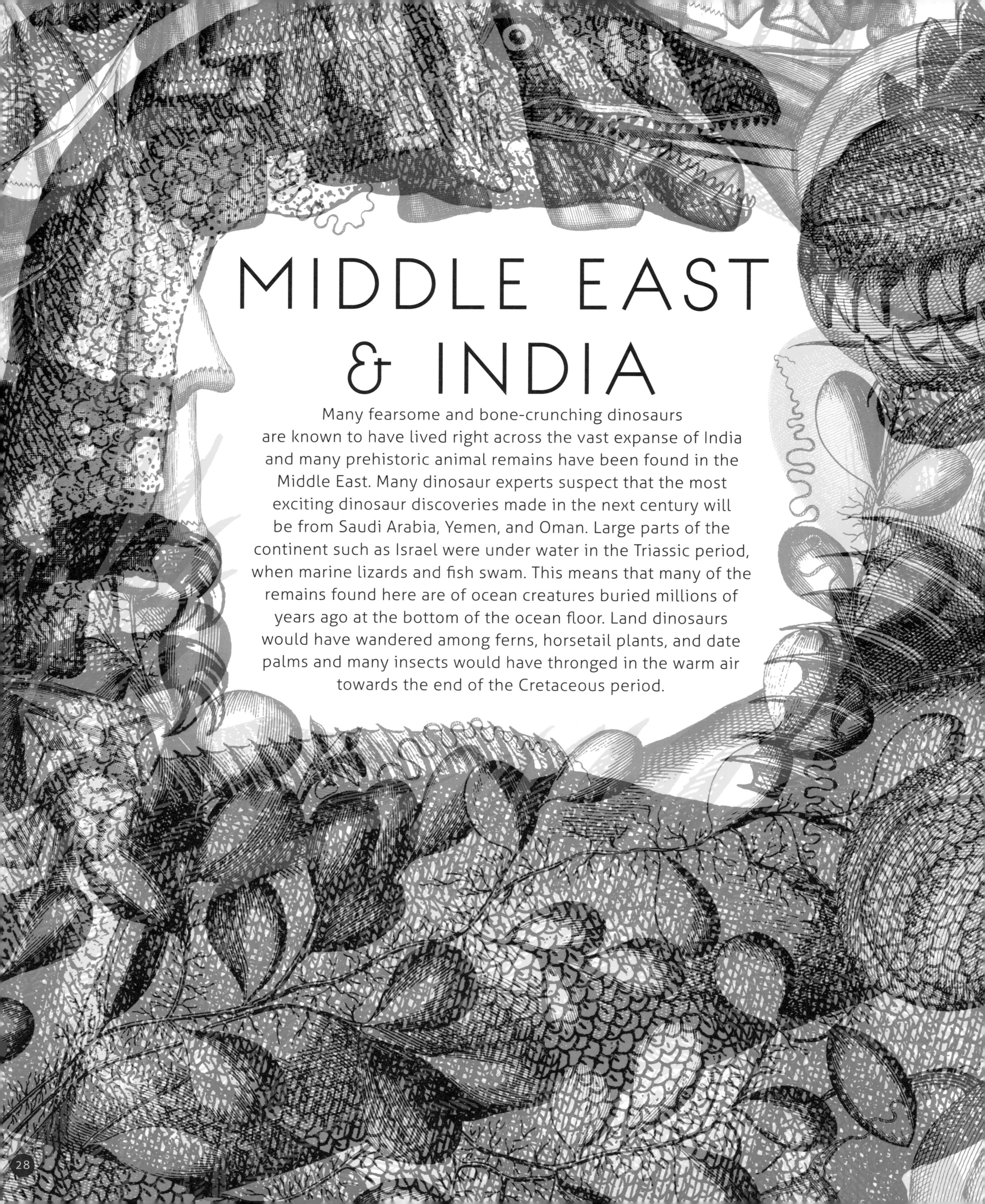

MIDDLE EAST & INDIA

Many fearsome and bone-crunching dinosaurs are known to have lived right across the vast expanse of India and many prehistoric animal remains have been found in the Middle East. Many dinosaur experts suspect that the most exciting dinosaur discoveries made in the next century will be from Saudi Arabia, Yemen, and Oman. Large parts of the continent such as Israel were under water in the Triassic period, when marine lizards and fish swam. This means that many of the remains found here are of ocean creatures buried millions of years ago at the bottom of the ocean floor. Land dinosaurs would have wandered among ferns, horsetail plants, and date palms and many insects would have thronged in the warm air towards the end of the Cretaceous period.

WELCOME TO THE
MIDDLE EAST & INDIA
1 9
7
6 3 4
2
5
8
DINOSAUR DISCOVERY SITES
1 Jaklapallisaurus, Madhya Pradesh, India
2 Alwalkeria, Andhra Pradesh, India
3 Kotasaurus, Telangana, India
4 Barapasaurus, Telangana, India
5 Lamplughsaurus, Andhra Pradesh, India
6 Isisaurus, Maharastra, India
7 Rajasaurus, Gujarat, India
8 Dravidosaurus, Tamil Nadu, India
9 Indosuchus, Madhya Pradesh, India

PREHISTROIC PLANTS AND ANIMALS

During the Cretaceous period, a warm shallow sea covered much of what we know to be the Middle East today. We have found extraordinary plants and ocean creatures buried under ancient silt and rock from this area. On land there would have been fruiting date palms, slithering snakes and varieties of pterosaurs perching in trees and swooping down on small mammals and fish.

READ about the plants and animals of the prehistoric Middle East and India, then turn back to the OBSERVATION DECK. Looking through the BLUE lens, what can you see?

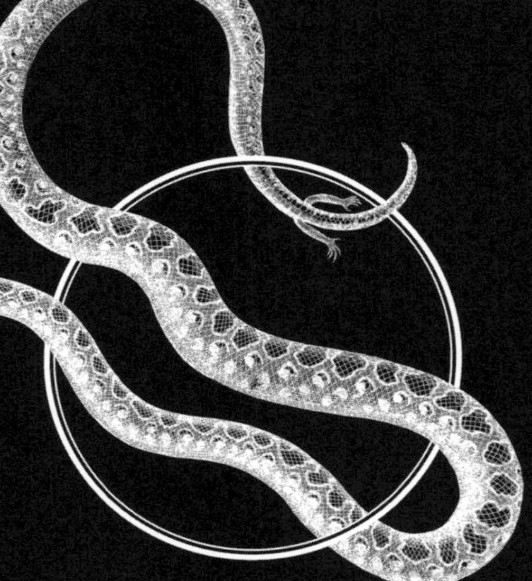

Pachyrhachis This looks like a snake but it has two tiny, tiny back legs and would have slithered across Israel.

Date palm A plant laden with sweet sticky date fruits and fans of foliage that would have cast welcome shade over the hot earth.

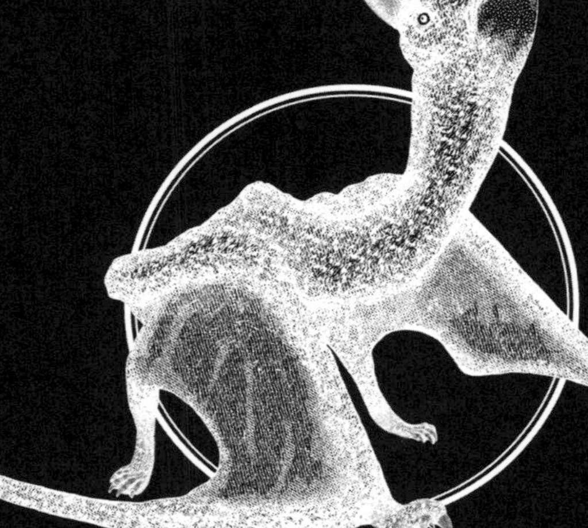

Arambourgiania A giant pterosaur that would have flown around the area we now call Jordan.

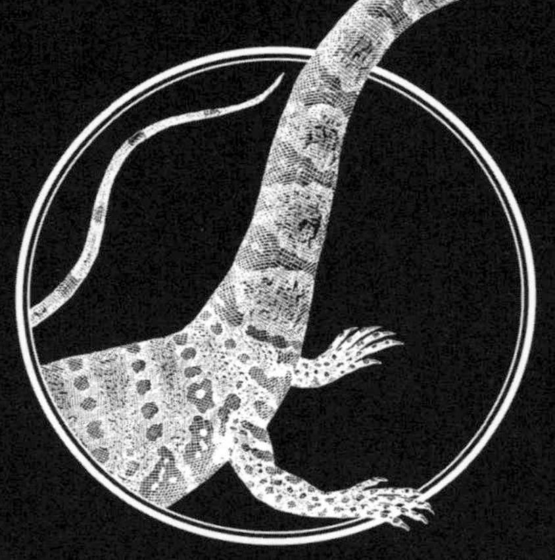

Tanystropheus A 6 metre-long lizard that looked a lot like a dinosaur. It lived in the Triassic period and was found in Saudi Arabia.

Aldabranus cabri These ducks would have survived the extinction event which wiped out dinosaurs at the end of the Cretaceous period.

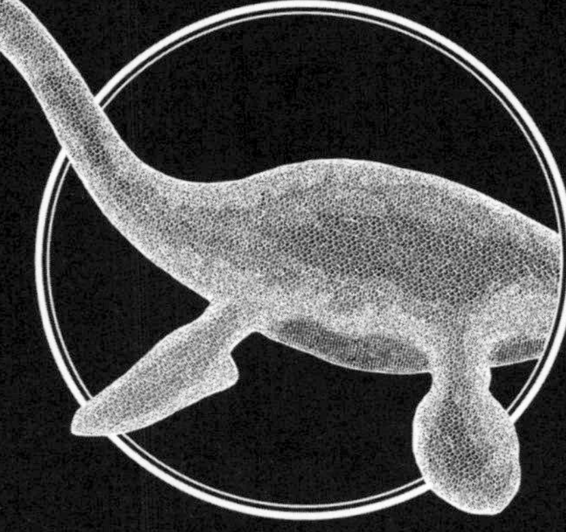

Elasmosaurus This huge ocean-faring reptile would have lived in the sea above the part of the earth we now call Israel.

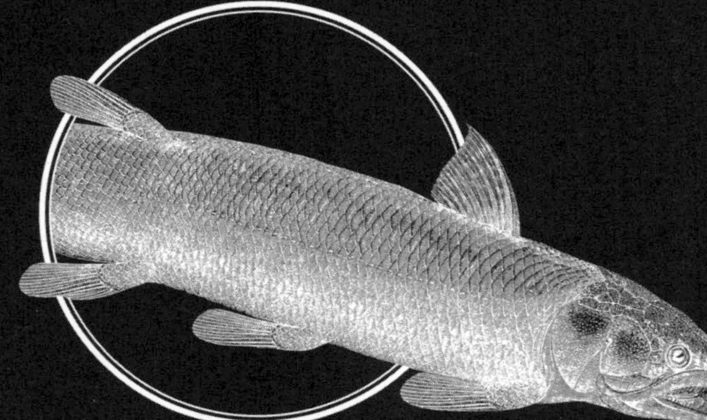

Coelacanth A nocturnal hunting fish that still swims in our oceans today. They can weigh up to a colossal 90 kilos.

Pluchea glutinosa An ancient species of flowering plant which only recently went extinct and was last found blooming in Yemen.

Protobrama This fish would have swum about in the oceans above Lebanon. It had a sleek, streamlined body.

DINOSAURS

India is a treasure trove of dinosaur discovery. The 230 million-year-old *Alwalkeria* kicked off dinosaur life here and the *Barapasaurus* wins the prize for the most complete skeleton. Many believe that the Middle East will likely contribute significantly to the next chapters of the dinosaur story, so watch this space...

READ about dinosaurs from different periods discovered in the Middle East and India. Then turn back to the OBSERVATION DECK. If you dare, look through the RED lens and come face to face with fearsome dinosaurs.

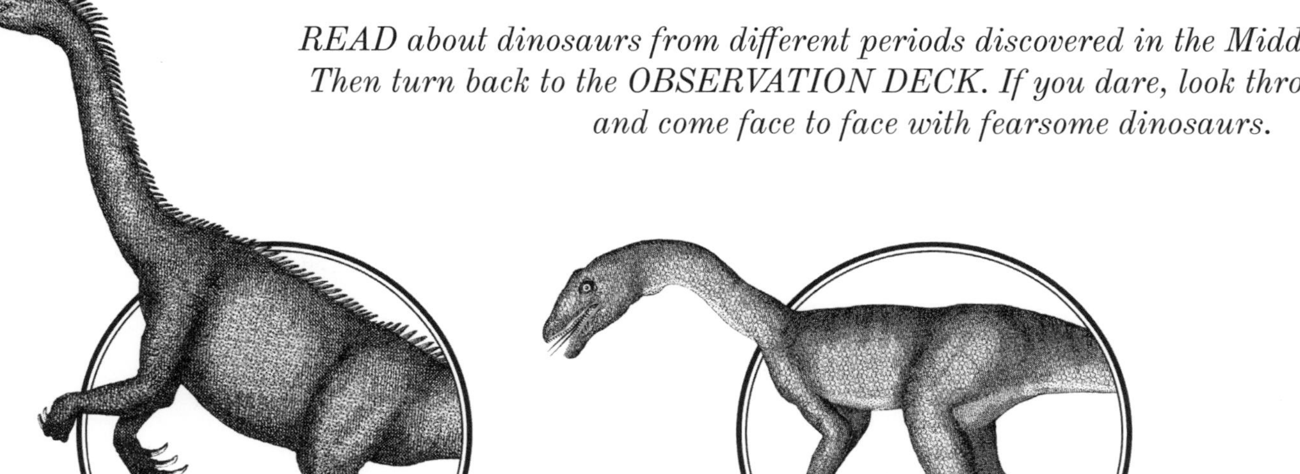

Triassic

Jaklapallisaurus, Jaklapalli Lizard, 217-201 MYA A medium-sized omnivore with a chunky tail and a squat neck compared to other sauropodomorphs.

Alwalkeria, for Alick Walker, 235-228 MYA This early dinosaur careered around on two legs and ate everything in its way, plant or animal.

Kotasaurus, Kota Lizard, 205-180 MYA This herbivorous sauropod was unusually big for its time.

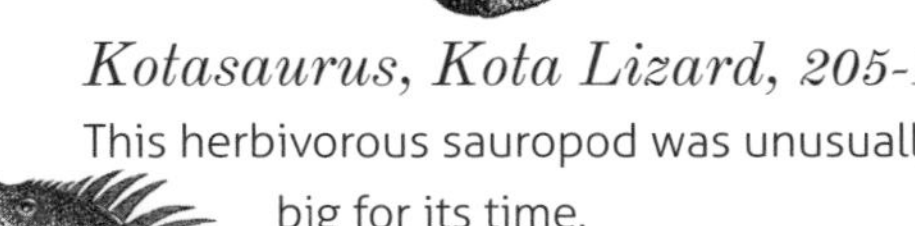

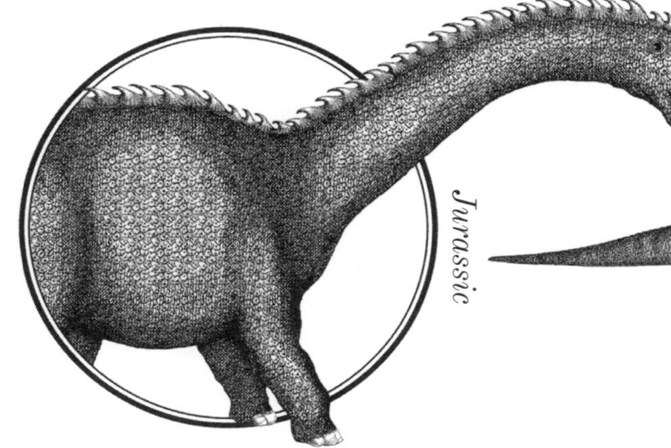

Jurassic

Barapasaurus, Big Leg Lizard, 185-170 MYA Found in India, this was a very big and early sauropod. At 45 foot tall it towered over most other creatures around it.

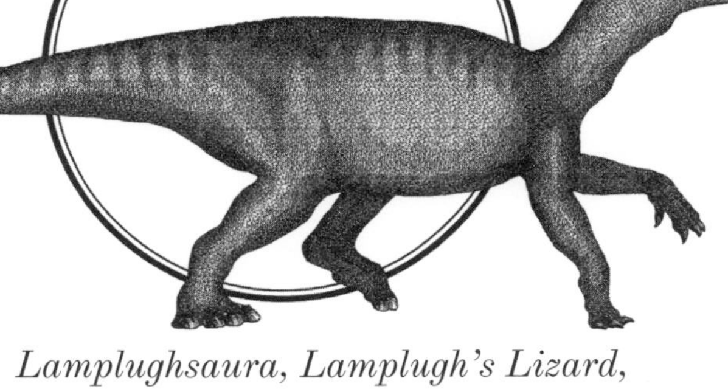

Jurassic

Lamplughsaura, Lamplugh's Lizard, 196-190 MYA Palaeontologists are not completely sure what family this 10 metre-long dinosaur belonged to.

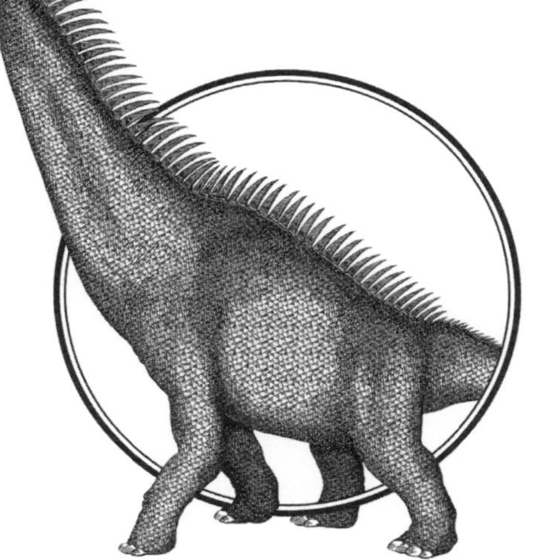

Cretaceous

Isisaurus, Indian Statistical Institute Lizard, 71-65 MYA This dinosaur was as tall as a modern-day giraffe. We know it loved to eat fungus because traces are in its fossilized poo.

Rajasaurus, King of Lizards, 72-66 MYA A low, rounded horn on the front of its skull make this regal meat-eater distinctive.

Dravidosaurus, Dravidanadu Lizard, 89-86 MYA This mysterious dinosaur causes scientists to argue, some think it is a marine reptile and some think it is a type of stegosaur.

Cretaceous

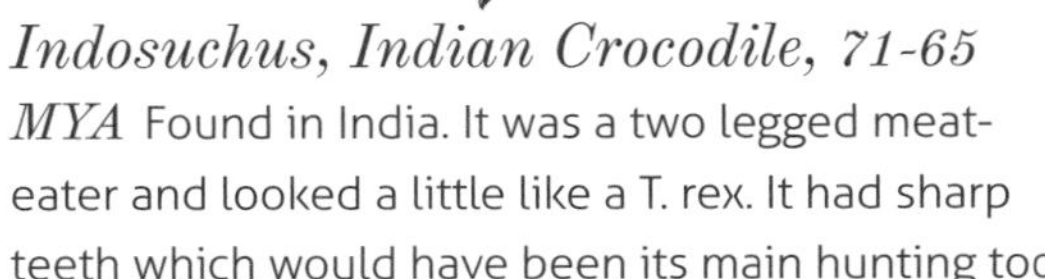

Indosuchus, Indian Crocodile, 71-65 MYA Found in India. It was a two legged meat-eater and looked a little like a T. rex. It had sharp teeth which would have been its main hunting tool.

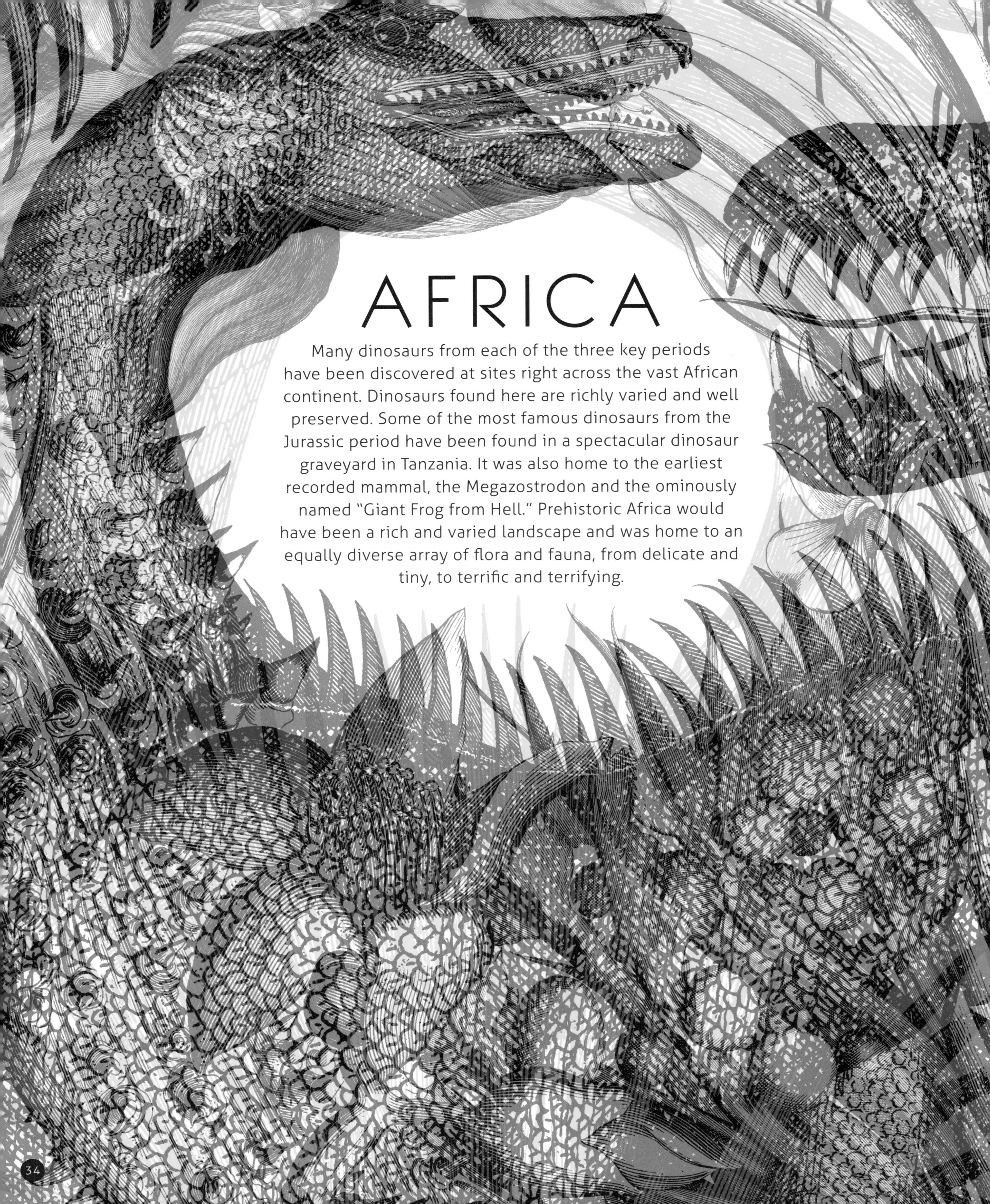

AFRICA

Many dinosaurs from each of the three key periods have been discovered at sites right across the vast African continent. Dinosaurs found here are richly varied and well preserved. Some of the most famous dinosaurs from the Jurassic period have been found in a spectacular dinosaur graveyard in Tanzania. It was also home to the earliest recorded mammal, the Megazostrodon and the ominously named "Giant Frog from Hell." Prehistoric Africa would have been a rich and varied landscape and was home to an equally diverse array of flora and fauna, from delicate and tiny, to terrific and terrifying.

WELCOME TO AFRICA
9
7
6
4
3
8
1
2
5
DINOSAUR DISCOVERY SITES
1 *Eocursor*, South Africa
2 *Heterodontosaurus*, Lesotho
3 *Massospondylus*, Zimbabwe
4 *Giraffatitan*, Tanzania
5 *Lesothosaurus*, Lesotho
6 *Elaphrosaurus*, Tanzania
7 *Afrovenator*, Niger
8 *Masiakasaurus*, Madagascar
9 *Spinosaurus*, Egypt

PREHISTORIC PLANTS AND ANIMALS

Africa is home to the earliest mammal discovered to date. It is a place of many firsts for the plant and animal kingdoms, from ocean, to land, to sky. Giant snakes would have slithered through the hot, damp tropical rainforests while colossal frogs chirruped, winged lizards soared overhead and heady pollen hung in the humid air.

READ about the plants and animals of prehistoric Africa, then turn back to the OBSERVATION DECK. Looking through the BLUE lens, what can you see?

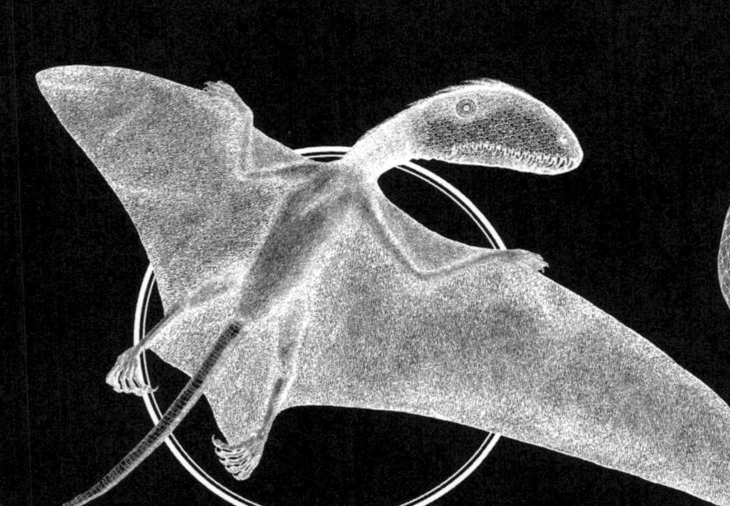

Dimorphodon A pterosaur with a head shaped like a puffin's. It was a rapid flier and cruised the skies, scooping up insects in its big mouth.

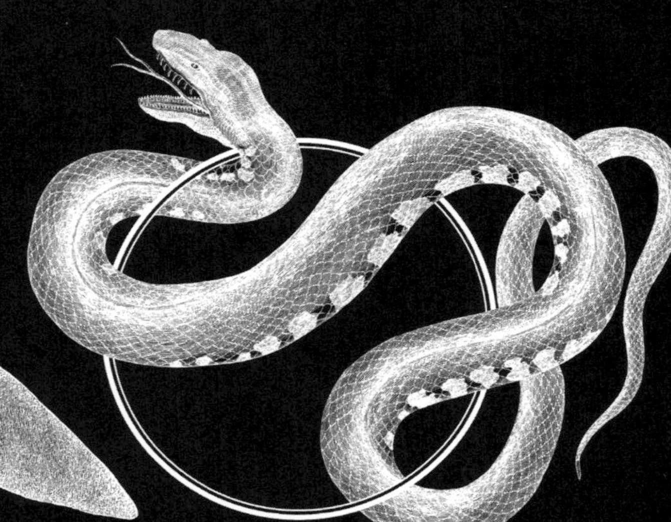

Madtsoia No one is quite sure how big these Cretaceous snakes grew but the largest ever found is over 30 foot long.

Beelzebufo frog, Giant Frog from Hell Thought to be very bad-tempered and aggressive, this frog weighed in at 4.5 kilos and ate lizards whole.

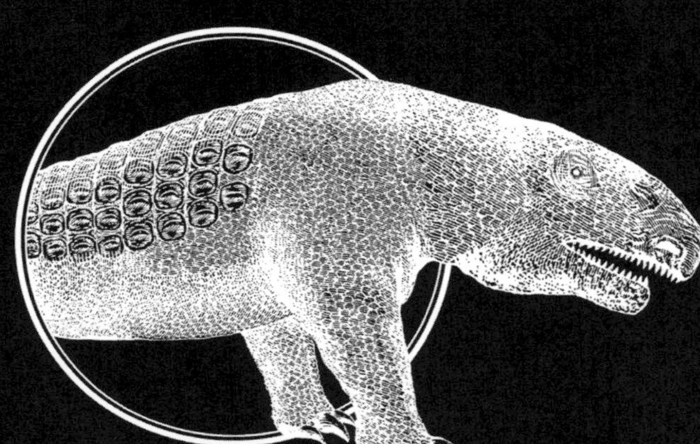

Erythrosuchus One of the largest land predators of the Triassic period, it had a big, powerful head and moved fast.

King protea This is the national flower of South Africa and has grown there for 80 million years, since the late Cretaceous period.

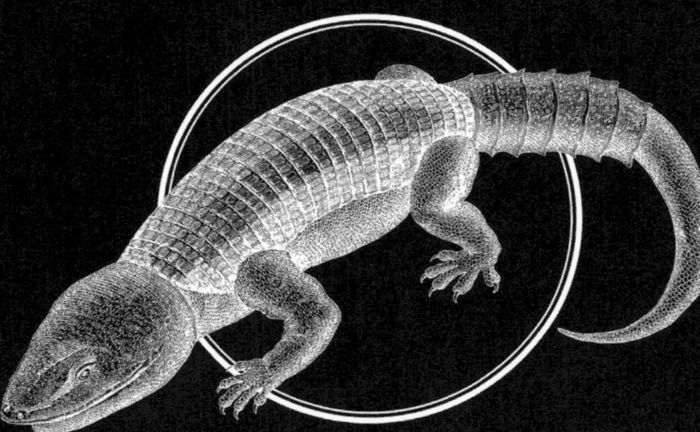

Peltobatrachus A slow-moving amphibian that lived on land, only returning to the water to lay its eggs. It mostly ate frogs, worms and snails.

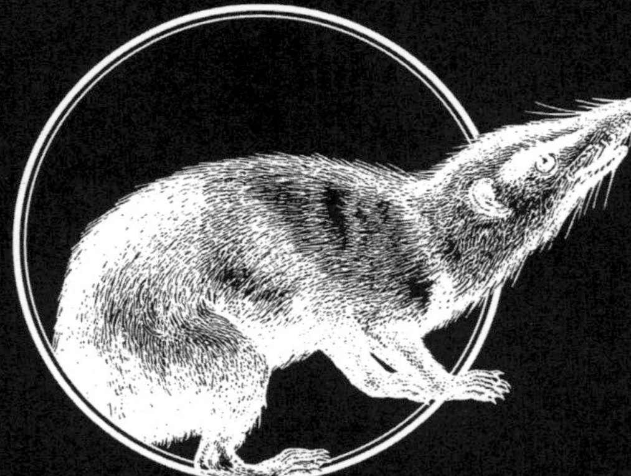

Megazostrodon Thought to be the earliest mammal ever found, it lived around 210 million years ago and hunted under the cover of night.

Allspice Dating from the late Cretaceous period, this flower still grows today and smells a little like bubblegum.

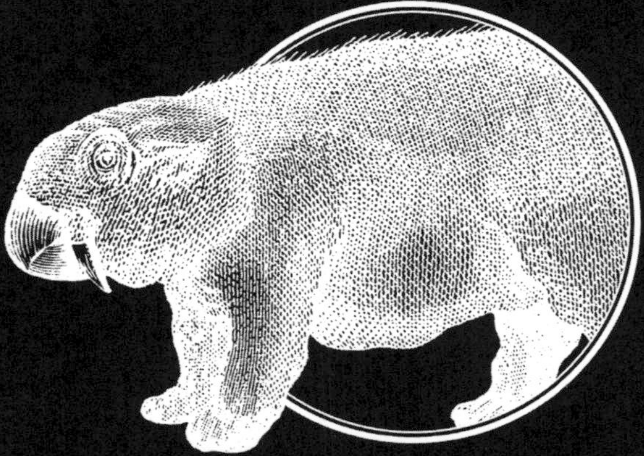

Lystrosaurus A pig-sized reptile with only two tusk-like teeth. It would have rootled around for small shrubs to munch with its beak-like jaw.

DINOSAURS

Some of the most important Jurassic discoveries have been made in the east of Africa at the Tanzanian Tendaguru Hill site. This dinosaur graveyard is one of many across the continent, which was once home to varied species of dinosaur from tiny plant-eaters, to master fishers to spiny, flesh-eating terrors.

READ about dinosaurs from different periods discovered in Africa. Then turn back to the OBSERVATION DECK. If you dare, look through the RED lens and come face to face with fearsome dinosaurs.

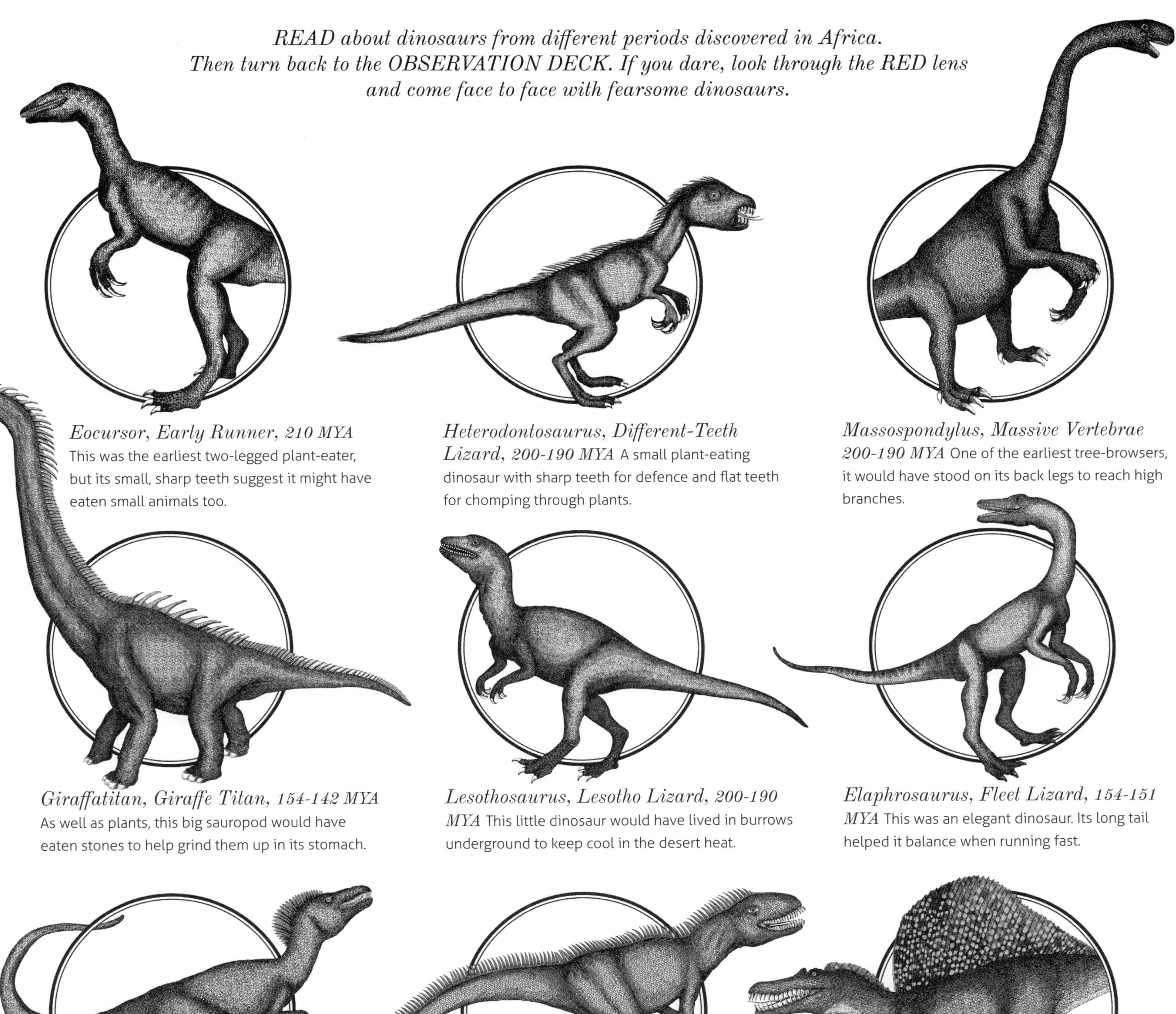

Triassic

Eocursor, Early Runner, 210 MYA This was the earliest two-legged plant-eater, but its small, sharp teeth suggest it might have eaten small animals too.

Heterodontosaurus, Different-Teeth Lizard, 200-190 MYA A small plant-eating dinosaur with sharp teeth for defence and flat teeth for chomping through plants.

Massospondylus, Massive Vertebrae 200-190 MYA One of the earliest tree-browsers, it would have stood on its back legs to reach high branches.

Jurassic

Giraffatitan, Giraffe Titan, 154-142 MYA As well as plants, this big sauropod would have eaten stones to help grind them up in its stomach.

Lesothosaurus, Lesotho Lizard, 200-190 MYA This little dinosaur would have lived in burrows underground to keep cool in the desert heat.

Elaphrosaurus, Fleet Lizard, 154-151 MYA This was an elegant dinosaur. Its long tail helped it balance when running fast.

Cretaceous

Afrovenator, African Hunter, 132-121 MYA Unfortunate prey would have stood no chance against the *Afrovenator's* razor-sharp claws.

Masiakasaurus, Vicious Lizard, 84-71 MYA Unusually, its front teeth pointed straight out in front rather than downwards, to help it catch fish.

Spinosaurus, Thorn Lizard, 95-70 MYA This fish-guzzling dinosaur thrived in Cretaceous Egypt, dense with tropical rainforest and teeming marshland.

NORTH AMERICA

This is a land home to some of the most famous dinosaurs ever discovered. The climate and rock in Utah, Wyoming, Montana and Colorado provide perfect environments to preserve these treasures from the past. Many dinosaur discoveries from all three periods, the Triassic, Jurassic and Cretaceous, have been made here. During the Cretaceous period, dinosaurs could have crossed between North America and Asia as the two were joined by a small strip of land. This is why North American dinosaurs share features with their Asian relatives. This continent is a true time capsule, rich with remains of dinosaur A-listers such as *T. rex*, *Triceratops* and *Brachiosaurus*. It was even home to some of the plants we still know and see today such as magnolias and tall redwood trees.

WELCOME TO NORTH AMERICA
7
8
5
9
4
3
2
6
1
DINOSAUR DISCOVERY SITES
1 *Daemonosaurus*, New Mexico, USA
2 *Tawa*, New Mexico, USA
3 *Gojirasaurus*, New Mexico, USA
4 *Brachiosaurus*, Colorado, USA
5 *Stegosaurus*, Utah, USA
6 *Ceratosaurus*, Oklahoma, USA
7 *Tyrannosaurus*, British Columbia, Canada
8 *Ankylosaurus*, Alberta, Canada
9 *Triceratops*, Colorado, USA

PREHISTORIC PLANTS AND ANIMALS

In the ever growing oceans and rivers of the Jurassic period, marine lizards thrived while the skies were thronging with swooping, shrieking pterosaurs. Many blooming plants from Cretaceous North America still thrive on the planet today, from the beautiful magnolia to the giant dawn redwoods that are famous in California.

READ about the plants and animals of prehistoric North America, then turn back to the OBSERVATION DECK. Looking through the BLUE lens, what can you see?

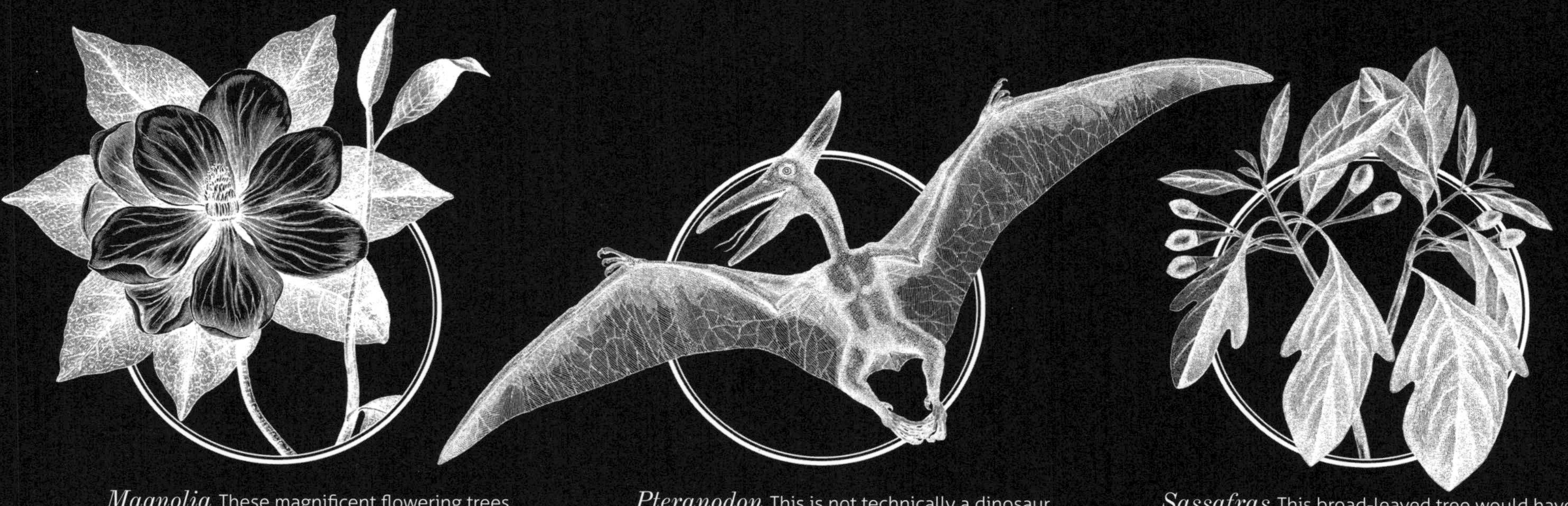

Magnolia These magnificent flowering trees started to bloom in the Cretaceous period, pollinated by beetles, bees and butterflies.

Pteranodon This is not technically a dinosaur, but a Cretaceous flying reptile. No one knows exactly why it has such a large crest on its head.

Sassafras This broad-leaved tree would have lined the planes of Cretaceous North America. It is still around today and used a lot in cooking.

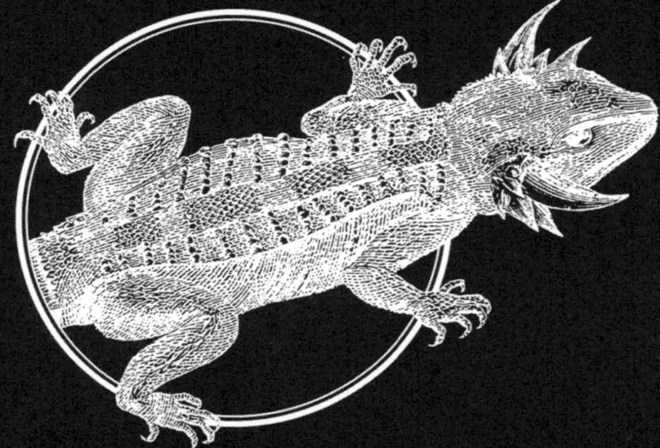

Hypsognathus Discovered in New Jersey, this ancient lizard would have mostly eaten insects and had unusual spikes at the corners of its skull.

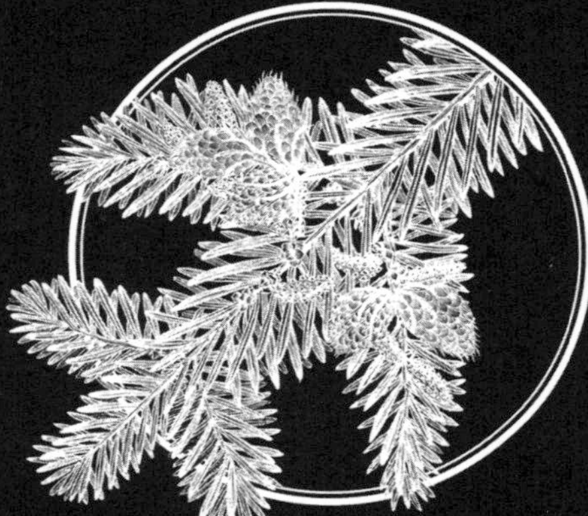

Dawn redwood These would have formed tall forests at the time *Triceratops* roamed. They could reach 60m tall, equivalent to a 13-storey building.

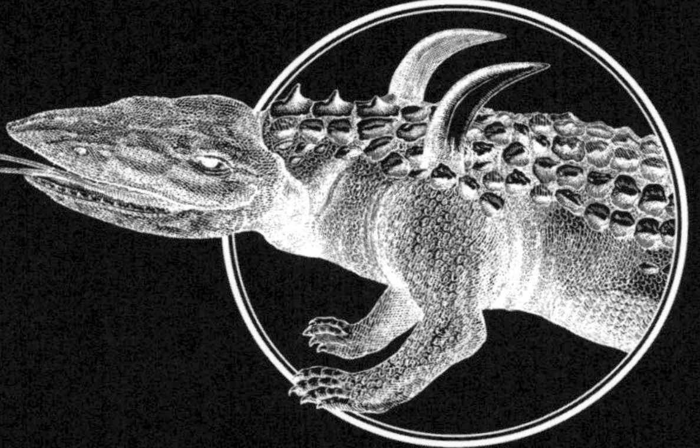

Desmatosuchus Found in Texas and from the Triassic period, this crocodile-like creature was more heavily armoured than *Ankylosaurus*—it even had armour under its tummy.

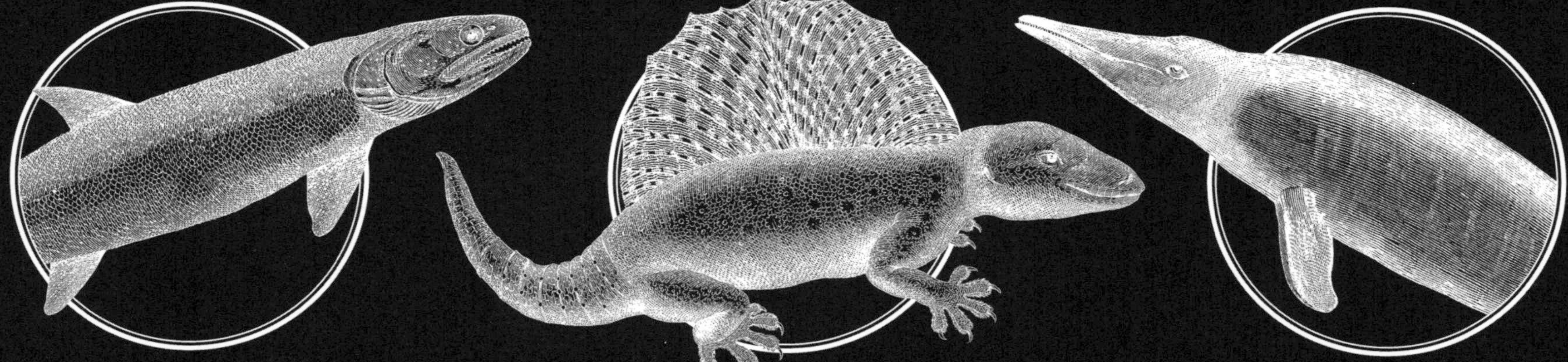

Eusthenopteron A prehistoric fish closely related to the first amphibians that crawled onto land. Its strong fins are like limbs but scientists agree it never truly emerged from the ocean.

Platyhystrix A small amphibian with a huge sail on its back. Because it was cold-blooded, scientists think the sail acted like a solar panel and caught the warmth from the sun as it basked.

Plotosaurus, Swimmer Lizard This marine lizard had a very streamlined body. We even have records of its skin texture which is similar to a modern-day shark.

DINOSAURS

Rich in fossils, Alberta in Canada and Dinosaur Ridge on the West Coast of the USA have yielded extraordinary dinosaur treasures. The most famous dinosaurs of the Mesozoic era were found here, including the king of the dinosaurs, the *Tyrannosaurus*, or *T. rex*.

READ about dinosaurs from different periods discovered in North America. Then turn back to the OBSERVATION DECK. If you dare, look through the RED lens and come face to face with fearsome dinosaurs.

Triassic

Daemonosaurus, Demon Lizard, 208-201 MYA This small dinosaur was unusual for having such a small head, short snout and bucked teeth.

Tawa, 215 MYA Named after a sun god, this little dinosaur was discovered in New Mexico and is a very early species of meat-eater.

Gojirasaurus, Godzilla Lizard, 228-209 MYA Its name is the Japanese word for Godzilla because it is unusually big for a Triassic dinosaur.

Jurassic

Brachiosaurus, Arm Lizard, 155-140 MYA Its long neck helped it nibble the tallest trees and because it had no competition it was always very well fed.

Stegosaurus, Roof Lizard, 156-144 MYA This big herbivore had diamond-shaped plates on its back. They may have been to warn off predators or to keep it cool by radiating out heat.

Ceratosaurus, Horned Lizard, 150-144 MYA The horn on its snout might have been used to signal danger to other dinosaurs. It mostly ate fish and crocodiles.

Cretaceous

Tyrannosaurus, Tyrant Lizard, 67-65 MYA This famous brute was a fearsome killer. It could easily crunch through bone with teeth and jaws three times as strong as a lion's.

Ankylosaurus, Stiff Lizard, 74-67 MYA A heavily armoured creature with a huge club tail. This dinosaur could cause serious damage, although this vegetarian was a fighter, not a hunter.

Triceratops, Three-horned Face, 67-65 MYA This famous dinosaur was built like a fighter tank. It had a huge protective neck frill, tough parrot-like beak and horns for fighting.

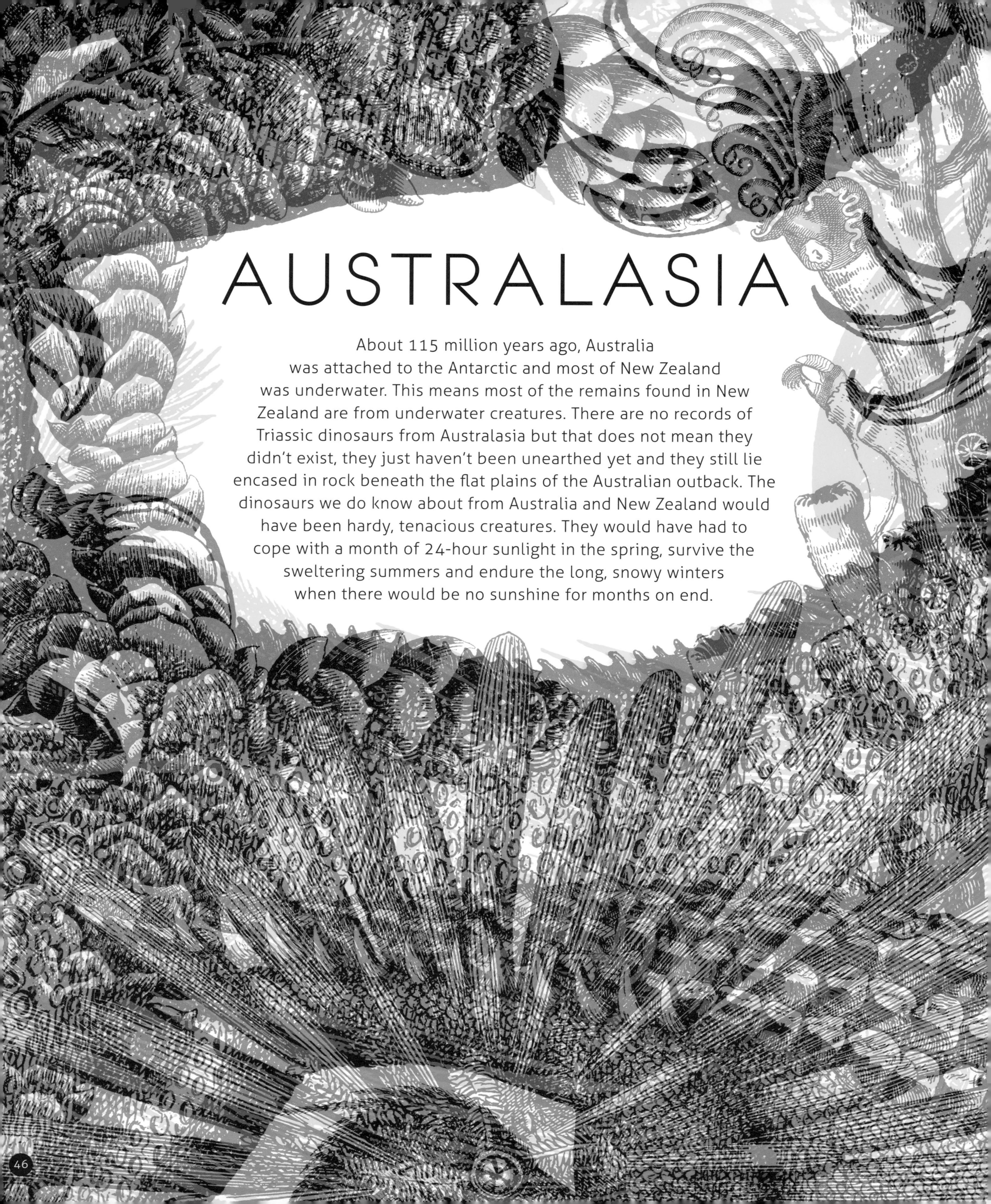

AUSTRALASIA

About 115 million years ago, Australia was attached to the Antarctic and most of New Zealand was underwater. This means most of the remains found in New Zealand are from underwater creatures. There are no records of Triassic dinosaurs from Australasia but that does not mean they didn't exist, they just haven't been unearthed yet and they still lie encased in rock beneath the flat plains of the Australian outback. The dinosaurs we do know about from Australia and New Zealand would have been hardy, tenacious creatures. They would have had to cope with a month of 24-hour sunlight in the spring, survive the sweltering summers and endure the long, snowy winters when there would be no sunshine for months on end.

DINOSAUR DISCOVERY SITES

1. *Rhoetosaurus*, Queensland, Australia
2. *Ozraptor*, Western Australia
3. *Qantassaurus*, Victoria, Australia
4. *Muttaburrasaurus*, Queensland, Australia
5. *Minmi*, Queensland, Australia
6. *Diluvicursor*, Victoria, Australia
7. *Diamantinasaurus*, New South Wales, Australia
8. *Leaellynasaura*, Victoria, Australia
9. *Australovenator*, Queensland, Australia

PREHISTORIC PLANTS AND ANIMALS

Many of the ocean creatures that swam around Mesozoic Australia settled to the bottom of the ocean. Over time they were interred, fossilized and some have now been excavated in a land we call New Zealand. The fertile ground of New Zealand and Australia provides huge insights into the plant and animal world of this splendid era.

READ about the plants and animals of prehistoric Australasia, then turn back to the OBSERVATION DECK. Looking through the BLUE lens, what can you see?

Bullockornis, demon duck of doom This monstrous bird lived after the dinosaurs had died out over 15 million years ago. At nearly 10 foot tall, its legs would have been as thick as tree trunks.

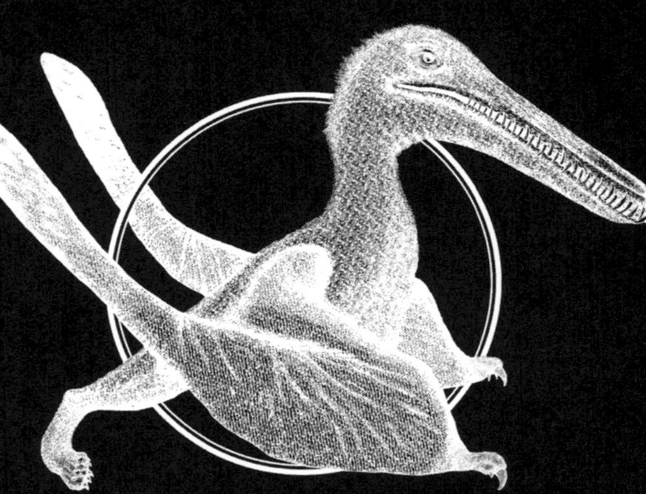

Mythunga This pterosaur would have soared above the coasts of Australia keeping a beady eye out for fish to swoop down on and eat.

Banksia A spectacular family of flowering plants that still grow in Australia today. They have distinctive feathery, brush-like flowers.

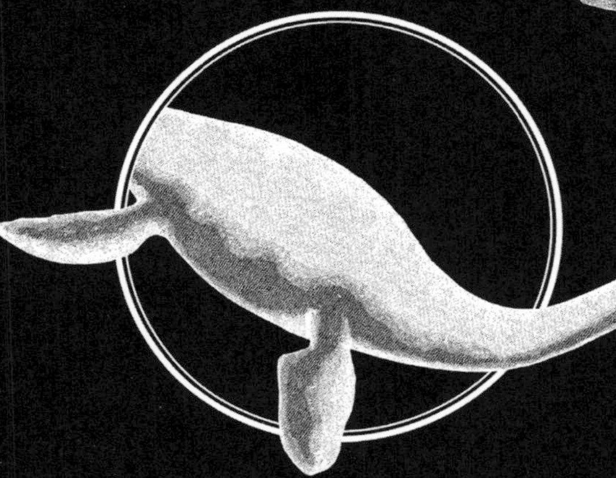

Kaiwhekea Discovered in New Zealand, this Cretaceous plessiosaur's name means "squid eater" in Māori.

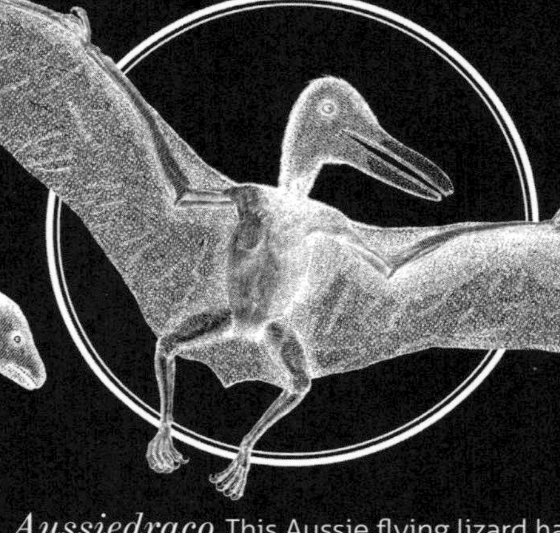

Aussiedraco This Aussie flying lizard had super sharp teeth and lived in the early Cretaceous period.

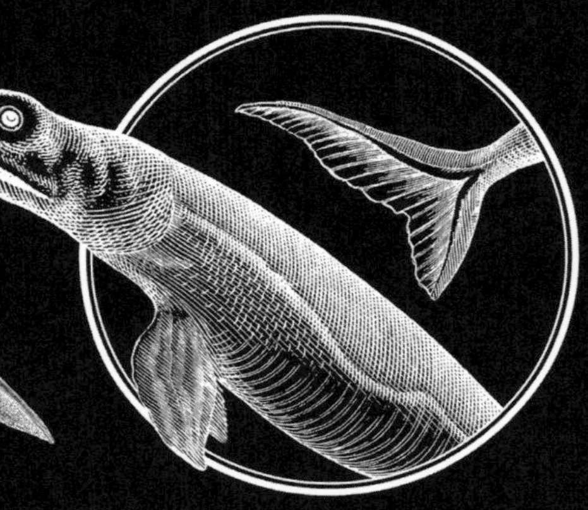

Taniwhasaurus From the mosasaur family which meant it was a ocean-dwelling lizard, its remains were unearthed in New Zealand.

Wollemi pine This tree is one of the oldest varieties in the world, it would have been around throughout the Mesozoic era.

Short-beaked echidna Still around today, unchanged since prehistoric times. They would have foraged on the forest floor for insects, while protected from danger by razor-sharp spines.

Giant's hare foot fern A creeping fern that still survives in the Australian outback. It would have blanketed the floor under dinosaurs' feet.

DINOSAURS

Welcome to Mesozoic Australasia, it is cold and it is often dark. When dinosaurs lived, Australia was much closer to the South Pole and so it was not the hot country we think of now. Dinosaurs would have adapted to cool temperatures and fewer hours of sunshine. Some dinosaurs like the little *Leaellynasaura* even had extra big eyes for seeing in low light and a downy, feathered body to keep it warm in the long cold nights.

READ about dinosaurs from different periods discovered in Australasia. Then turn back to the OBSERVATION DECK. If you dare, look through the RED lens and come face to face with fearsome dinosaurs.

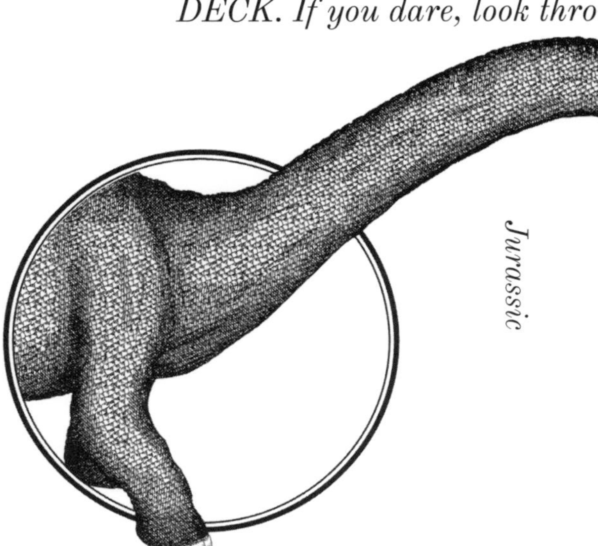

Jurassic

Rhoetosaurus, Rhoetos Lizard, 177-169 MYA Named after the Greek giant Rhoetus, this dinosaur weighed in at 20 tonnes—it would have had to eat a lot of leaves to stay full!

Jurassic

Ozraptor, Australian Thief, 170 MYA Only one of these dinosaurs has ever been uncovered and it was on the Western Australian coast. It was a small meat-eater with long back legs.

Cretaceous

Qantassaurus, Qantas Lizard, 122-112 MYA Named after the airline Qantas, this herbivore had a small jaw and only ten cheekteeth for munching shrubs such as horsetails and ferns.

Muttaburrasaurus, Muttaburra Lizard, 110-100 MYA It honked its fleshy nose flap to chat with others in its herd. The more inflated the nose flap, the more attractive it was to females!

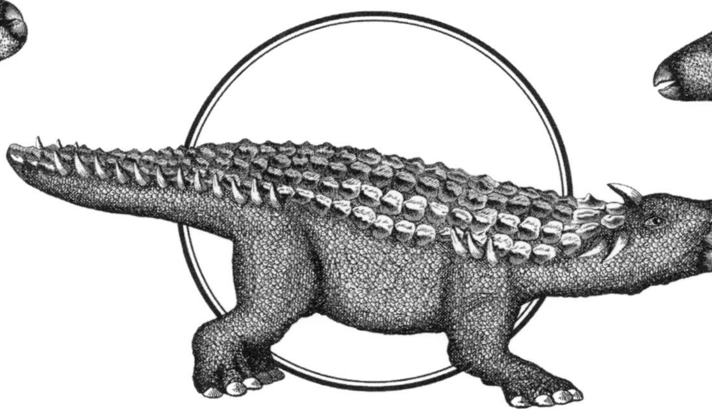

Minmi, for the Minmi river crossing, 121-112 MYA It looked like a mini Ankylosaurus. Its tough spikes made up for it being too slow to flee danger.

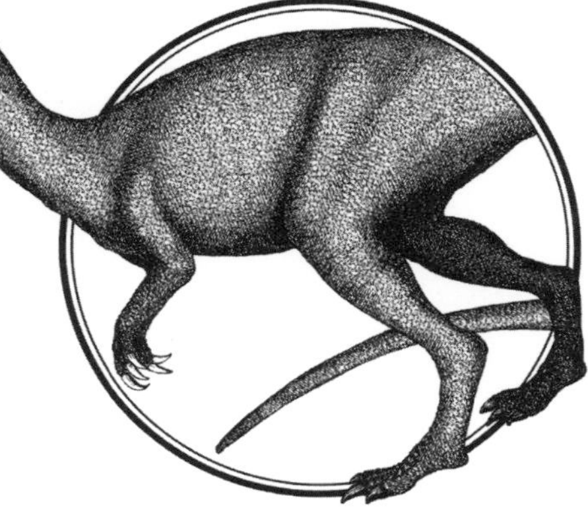

Cretaceous

Diluvicursur, Flood Runner, 115-110 MYA A small plant-eating dinosaur, about the size of a turkey—not all dinosaurs were huge!

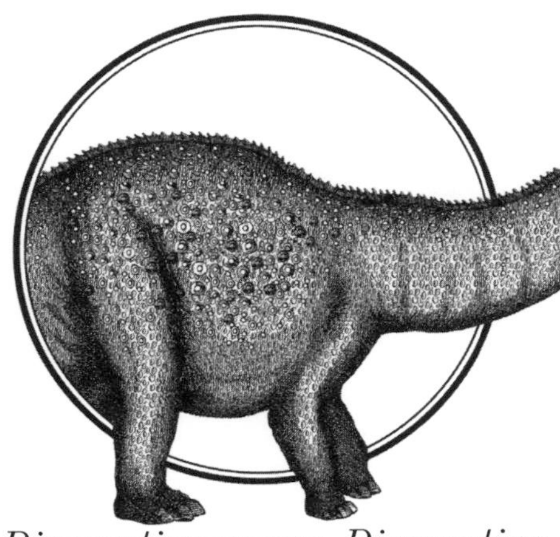

Diamantinasaurus, Diamantina River Lizard, 94-90 MYA This titanosaur weighed as much as a hippo. Fossilized footprints exist from when it tramped along the Queensland coastline.

Leaellynasaura, Leaellyn's Lizard, 115-110 MYA A little feathered dinosaur with an extra-long tail. It is thought that it used its tail to wrap around itself to stay warm in the polar forests.

Australovenator, Southern Hunter, 95 MYA It was a lightweight, fast runner which is why it is sometimes called "the cheetah of its time."

ANTARCTICA

Antarctica was once joined to Australia and South America in a supercontinent called Gondwana. It only started to break apart at the end of the Cretaceous period—long after Pangaea had split apart. We think of Antarctica as frozen and desolate but in prehistoric times it would have been lush, green woodland. We know it would have been cold here for part of the year because some trees had extra thick "skin" on the pine needles to stop them from freezing. The many dinosaurs that would have lived here are now buried under deep permafrost so very few are known about. Discoveries here take a long time to unearth—or un-ice! The first dinosaur uncovered took a team 10 years, all the while battling against the biting Antarctic winds and snow.

WELCOME TO ANTARCTICA
5
3
4
6
1
2
DINOSAUR DISCOVERY SITES
1 Glacialisaurus, Mount Kirkpatrick, Antarctica
2 Crylophosaurus, Mount Kirkpatrick, Antarctica
3 Carnotaurus, James Ross Island, Antarctica
4 Antarctopelta, James Ross Island, Antarctica
5 Trinisaura, James Ross Island, Antarctica
6 Morrosaurus, Snow Hill Island, Antarctica

PREHISTORIC PLANTS AND ANIMALS

Parts of Antarctica would have been underwater during the Mesozoic era and so the creatures we find there are often ocean creatures that sunk to the bottom of the ocean floor when they died. Scientists have also uncovered hoards of frozen seeds and plant matter which help us build up a picture of a beautifully forested land.

READ about the plants and animals of prehistoric Antarctica, then turn back to the OBSERVATION DECK. Looking through the BLUE lens, what can you see?

Saurichthys A long, narrow hunting fish that would lurk in long reeds, ambush and then brutally attack its startled prey.

Crinoid Like a kind of sea cucumber, this basic life form would catch tiny prey in its feathery frond-like arms in the oceans around Antarctica.

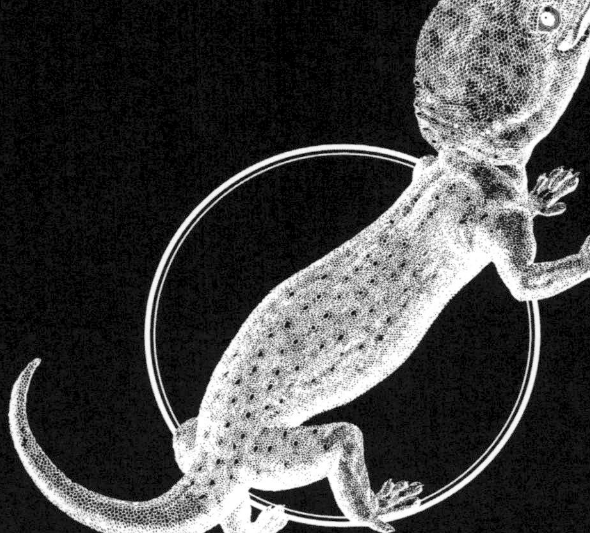

Koolasuchus This amphibian may look like a tadpole but it was big enough to eat small dinosaurs whole and that is exactly what it did.

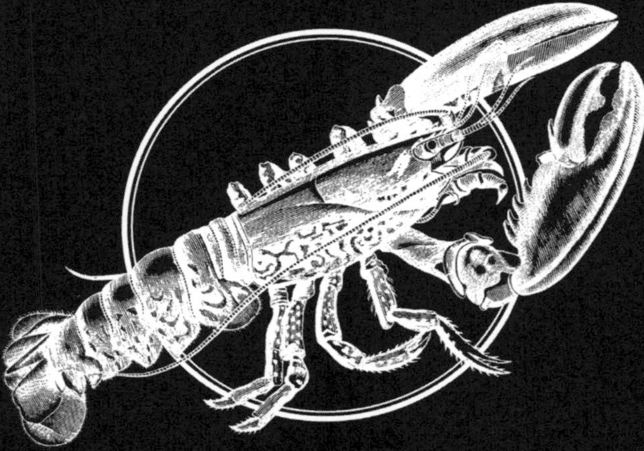

Hoploparia This lobster looks much like the ones that live now. It lived in the Jurassic period and had big heavy claws for defending itself.

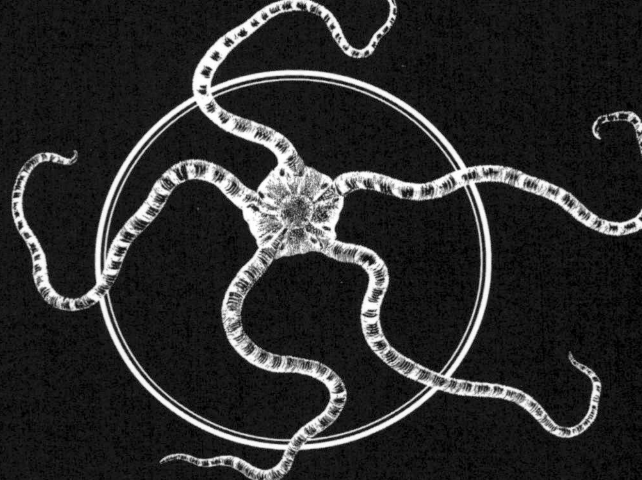

Ophiura A species of brittlestar fish with long, elegant limbs and a circular central body. It is still found today.

Polarornis A type of bird that looked a little like a duck and lived during the Cretaceous period. Its fossil was found on Seymour Island in Antarctica

Osteolepis This fish was very unusual, its body was covered in special cells that could sense vibrations or dangerous chemicals and would help it escape danger.

Dicksonia Antarctica tree fern A feathery, evergreen fern that would have added texture to the forests of Cretaceous Antarctica.

Kaikaifilu A 10 metre-long mosasaur would have patroled the oceans around Antarctic islands hunting plesiosaurs.

DINOSAURS

Beaming ourselves back to Mesozoic Antarctica requires a bit more imagination than with most other places. The ground holding the secrets to the dinosaur past is largely locked away under permafrost. But we do know that Antarctica was attached to mainland Australia for the whole time dinosaurs lived and so we have a very good idea of what most likely lived there. Some Antarctic dinosaurs have been found, but others are very likely suspects that we know for certain roamed Australia.

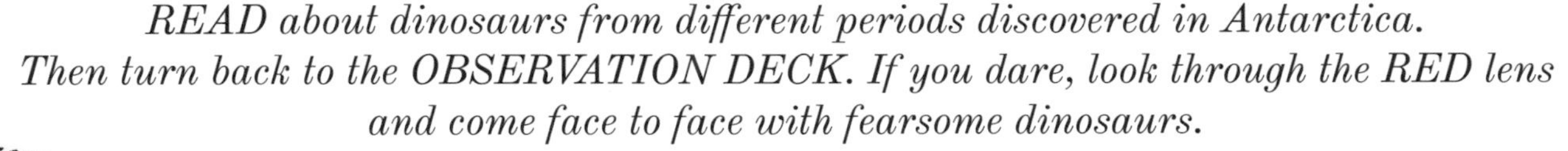

READ about dinosaurs from different periods discovered in Antarctica. Then turn back to the OBSERVATION DECK. If you dare, look through the RED lens and come face to face with fearsome dinosaurs.

Jurassic

Glacialisaurus, Glacier Lizard, 199-185 MYA An early plant-eater, with nearest relatives in South America and China; but the only fossils are a foot and parts of the leg.

Crylophosaurus, Frozen-Crested Lizard, 170 MYA This dinosaur is nicknamed *Elvisaurus* for its strange head crest, which looks a little bit like the quiff of the king of rock and roll.

Cretaceous

Carnotaurus, Carnivorous Bull, 70 MYA Originally discovered in Argentina in South America, remains of this terrifying meat-eater were also uncovered in Antarctica in 2003.

Antarctopelta, Antarctic Shield, 99-94 MYA This was the first dinosaur found in Antarctica. The harsh weather and frozen ground meant it took 10 years to uncover it.

Trinisaura, 70 MYA A tiny plant-eater that would have scurried around looking for leaves to snaffle while trying to hide from bigger carnivores.

Morrosaurus, El Morro Lizard, 70 MYA A small sauropod that would have been a meat-eater and scavenged when it couldn't find prey.

SOUTH AMERICA

This is a continent that is rich with prehistoric stories still waiting to be uncovered. Many palaeontologists believe that the first dinosaurs originated in South America. That is because the remains of some of the oldest dinosaurs ever discovered, including *Mussasaurus* and *Eodromaeus* have been found here. When the continents were all joined in one landmass called Pangaea, South America was attached to Africa, and so many dinosaurs that lived here have also been found in Africa. Argentina, in the south of the continent, has been home to many dinosaur discoveries of huge importance, including perfectly fossilized and preserved dinosaur eggs and the biggest dinosaur ever discovered, the *Argentinosaurus*, named after the country in which it was unearthed.

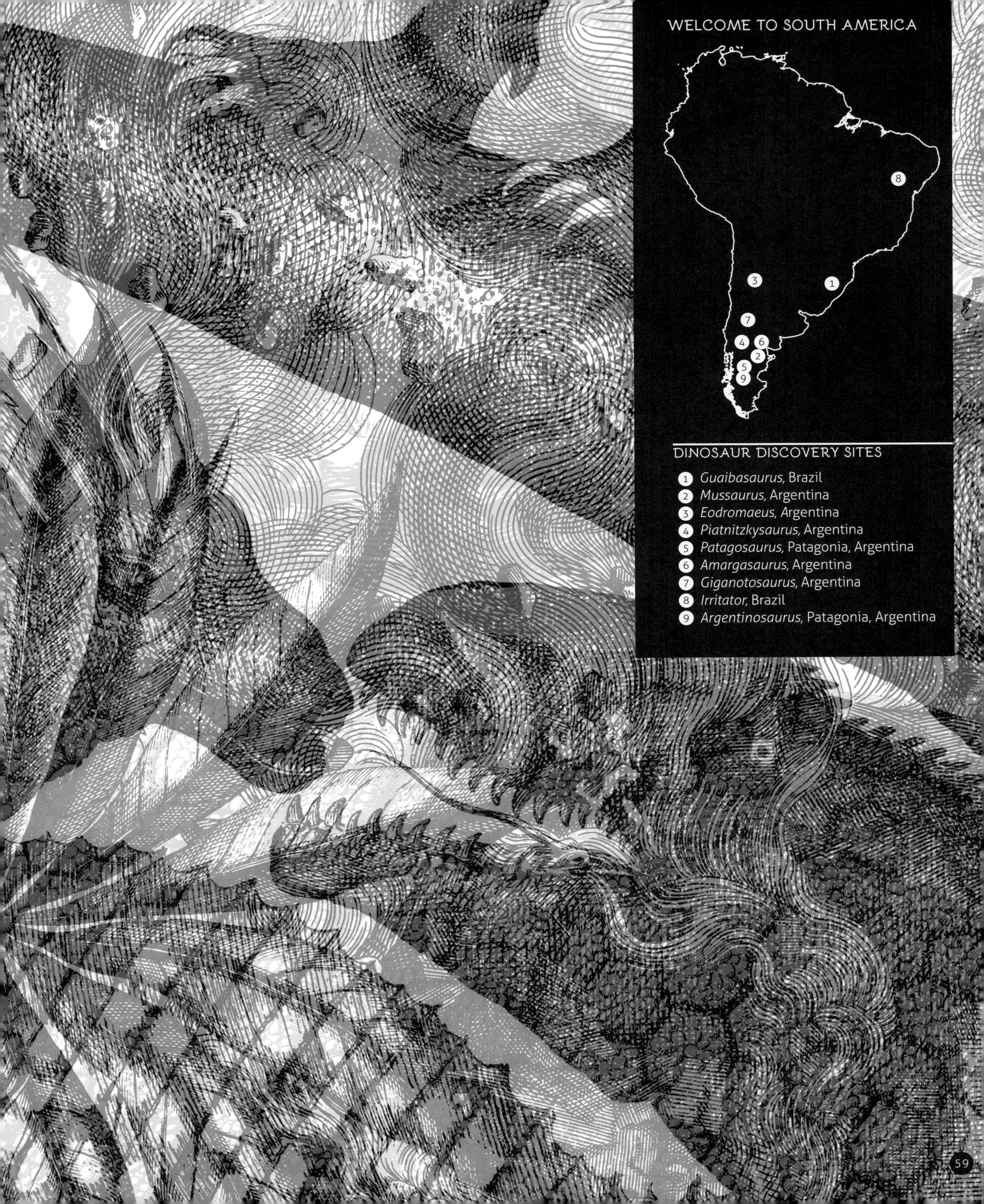

WELCOME TO SOUTH AMERICA
8
3
1
7
4
6
2
5
9
DINOSAUR DISCOVERY SITES
1 *Guaibasaurus*, Brazil
2 *Mussaurus*, Argentina
3 *Eodromaeus*, Argentina
4 *Piatnitzkysaurus*, Argentina
5 *Patagosaurus*, Patagonia, Argentina
6 *Amargasaurus*, Argentina
7 *Giganotosaurus*, Argentina
8 *Irritator*, Brazil
9 *Argentinosaurus*, Patagonia, Argentina

PREHISTORIC PLANTS AND ANIMALS

Travel back millions of years to a place we now call South America and see the ancestors of some plants and creatures you may recognize from the world we live in today. Spot fungi horns the size of trees and see hopping micro-kangaroos. Ancestors of bees and armadillos once roamed the tropical fern-blanketed landscapes of South America.

READ about the plants and animals of prehistoric South America, then turn back to the OBSERVATION DECK. Looking through the BLUE lens, what can you see?

Black pepper Originally from Cretaceous Colombia, this piquant plant is something we still season our food with today.

Cycad These spiky-leaved plants have been around for 280 million years and have survived several mass extinctions.

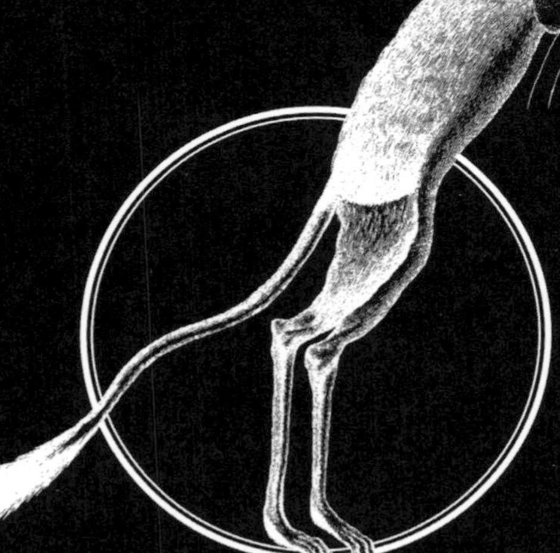

Argyrolagus A tiny marsupial that looked like a miniature modern-day kangaroo, even though it was not related at all.

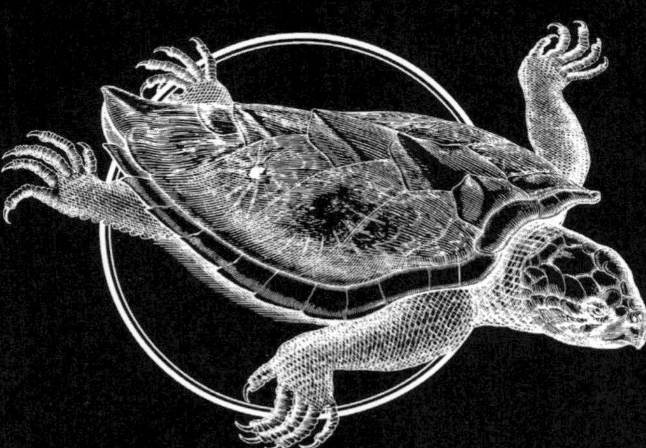

Stupendemys At 7.7 feet long, this was the largest freshwater turtle ever. It only became extinct relatively recently—3 million years ago.

Bees These-all important insects lived 100 million years ago and helped to pollinate late Cretaceous flowering plants.

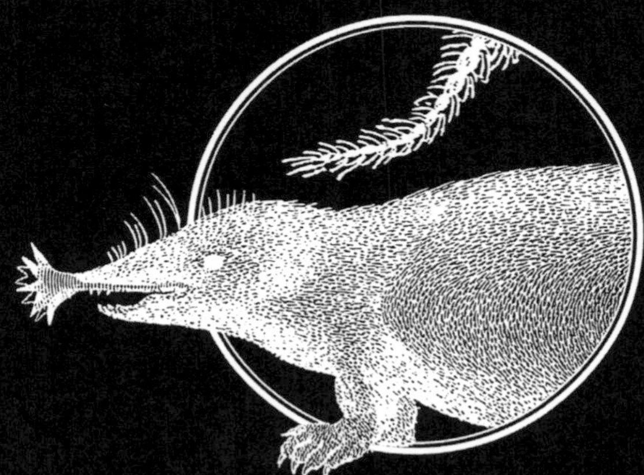

Necrolestes A mole-like tentacle-snouted mammal. It ate worms that feed on decaying things which is how it gets its name, meaning "grave robber."

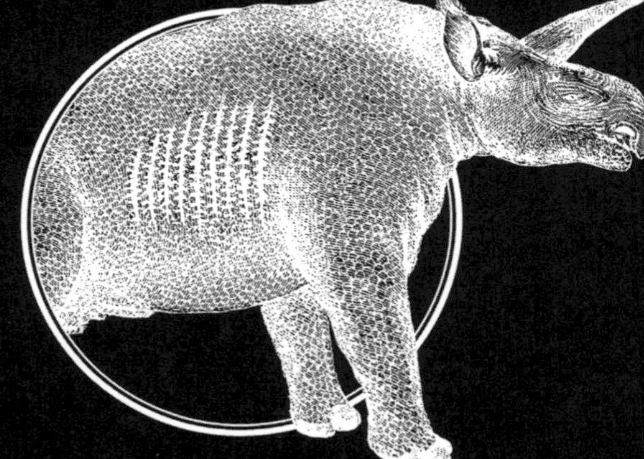

Hoffstetterius Dating back 66 million years these creatures look a lot like modern rhinos and were eventually hunted by early humans.

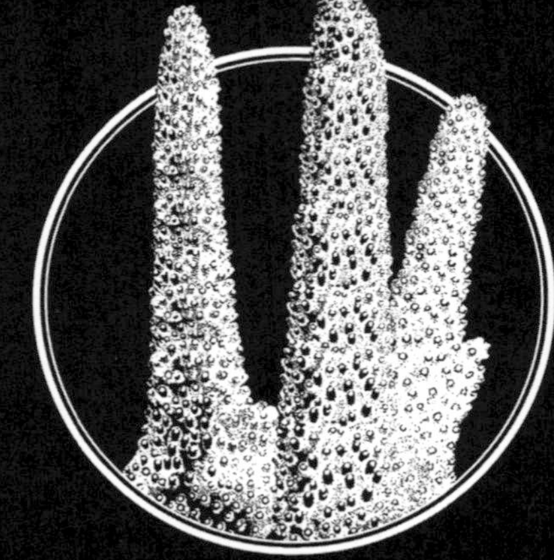

Prototaxites A type of giant fungus from over 350 million years ago. They would have towered over any other living thing around them.

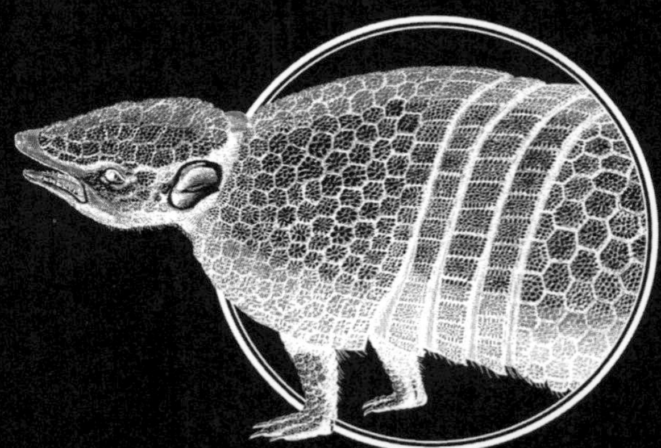

Pampatherian A prehistoric relative of the armadillo, this armored mammal lived after the dinosaurs became extinct in South America.

DINOSAURS

South America has provided rich pickings for palaeontologists for many years. The ideal combinations of climate, humidity rock and soil in different regions has perfectly preserved some of the continents most spectacular dinosaurs. From the smallest to the biggest, South America has seen many record-breaking dinosaur discoveries.

READ about dinosaurs from different periods discovered in South America. Then turn back to the OBSERVATION DECK. If you dare, look through the RED lens and come face to face with fearsome dinosaurs.

Triassic

Guaibasaurus, Rio Guaiba Lizard, 221-210 MYA A herbivore whose remains were discovered near the Rio Grande river in Brazil.

Mussaurus, Mouse Lizard, 221-220 MYA The first one of its kind to be uncovered was very tiny and so it was called the Mouse Lizard.

Eodromaeus, Dawn Runner, 230 MYA This little carnivore could run like the wind which is where it gets its nickname, the Dawn Runner.

Jurassic

Piatnitzkysaurus, Piatnitzky's Lizard, 164-159 MYA Standing at the same height as a human, this predator was a fast and vicious killer.

Jurassic

Patagosaurus, Patagonian Lizard, 164-159 MYA This 18 metre-long, hungry herbivore stripped tens of trees a day with its peg-shaped teeth.

Cretaceous

Amargasaurus, Amarga Lizard, 132-127 MYA Scientists think the spines that grew from its backbone supported fans of skin which shed heat.

Cretaceous

Giganotosaurus, Giant Southern Lizard, 112-90 MYA This huge dinosaur looked a lot like a *T. rex* but was much bigger and lived millions of years earlier than its famous cousin.

Irritator, 112-100 MYA This dinosaur didn't have an annoying character. Instead, palaeontologists named it because its scattered, fossilized remains made it a tricky beast to classify.

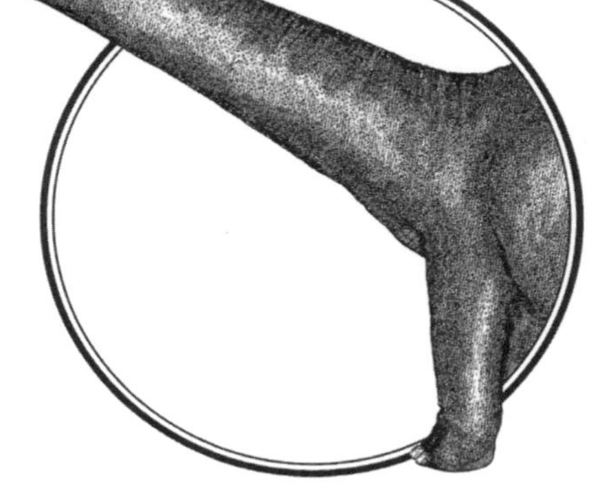

Argentinosaurus, Argentina Lizard, 90 MYA A vegetarian giant and the largest land animal ever found. In its lifetime, it never stopped growing. The largest ever found is 115 feet long.

Scan the code to turn your device into a magic three color lens.

Brimming with creative inspiration, how-to projects, and useful information to enrich your everyday life, Quarto Knows is a favorite destination for those pursuing their interests and passions. Visit our site and dig deeper with our books into your area of interest: Quarto Creates, Quarto Cooks, Quarto Homes, Quarto Lives, Quarto Drives, Quarto Explores, Quarto Gifts, or Quarto Kids.

Written by Lucy Brownridge

First Published in 2020 by Wide Eyed Editions, an imprint of The Quarto Group.
100 Cummings Center, Suite 265D, Beverly, MA 01915, USA.
T +1 978-282-9590 F +1 978-283-2742 **www.QuartoKnows.com**

A catalogue record for this book is available from the British Library.

ISBN 978-0-7112-5250-9
The illustrations were created digitally
Set in Aller Light, Bellota and Old Standard

Published by Georgia Amson-Bradshaw
Designed by Myrto Dimitrakoulia
Edited by Lucy Brownridge
Production by Chris Tucker
Consultant Professor Michael Benton
Manufactured in ShaoGuan, China SL112020

9 8 7 6 5 4 3 2